NIHIKÉYAH

Navajo Homeland

EDITED BY LLOYD L. LEE

THE UNIVERSITY OF
ARIZONA PRESS

TUCSON

The University of Arizona Press
www.uapress.arizona.edu

We respectfully acknowledge the University of Arizona is on the land and territories of Indigenous peoples. Today, Arizona is home to twenty-two federally recognized tribes, with Tucson being home to the O'odham and the Yaqui. Committed to diversity and inclusion, the University strives to build sustainable relationships with sovereign Native Nations and Indigenous communities through education offerings, partnerships, and community service.

ISBN-13: 978-0-8165-5225-2 (hardcover)
ISBN-13: 978-0-8165-5224-5 (paperback)
ISBN-13: 978-0-8165-5226-9 (ebook)

Cover design by Leigh McDonald
Cover art by Venaya Yazzie
Typeset by Sara Thaxton in 10.5/14 Adobe Text Pro with Trajan Sans Pro

Publication of this book is made possible in part by the proceeds of a permanent endowment created with the assistance of a Challenge Grant from the National Endowment for the Humanities, a federal agency.

Library of Congress Cataloging-in-Publication Data
Names: Lee, Lloyd L., 1971– editor.
Title: Nihikéyah : Navajo homeland / edited by Lloyd L. Lee.
Description: Tucson : University of Arizona Press, 2023. | Includes bibliographical references and index.
Identifiers: LCCN 2022061271 (print) | LCCN 2022061272 (ebook) | ISBN 9780816552252 (hardcover) | ISBN 9780816552245 (paperback) | ISBN 9780816552269 (ebook)
Subjects: LCSH: Navajo philosophy. | Navajo Indians—Social life and customs. | Navajo Nation, Arizona, New Mexico & Utah.
Classification: LCC E99.N3 N527 2023 (print) | LCC E99.N3 (ebook) | DDC 979.1004/9726—dc23/eng/20230126
LC record available at https://lccn.loc.gov/2022061271
LC ebook record available at https://lccn.loc.gov/2022061272

Printed in the United States of America
♾ This paper meets the requirements of ANSI/NISO Z39.48-1992 (Permanence of Paper).

CONTENTS

NÁHOOKQS/ NORTH

NIHIKÉYAH

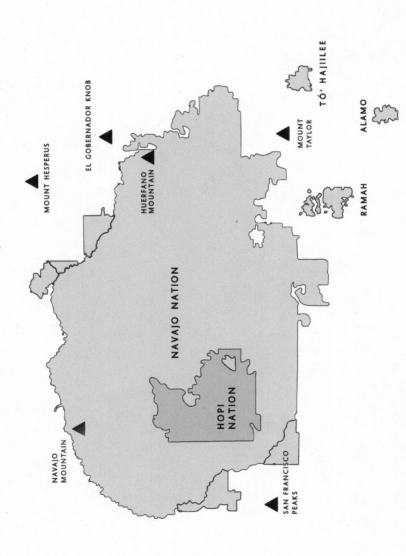

MOUNT BLANCA

TÓ' HAJIILEE

EL GOBERNADOR KNOB

MOUNT HESPERUS

HUERFANO MOUNTAIN

MOUNT TAYLOR

ALAMO

RAMAH

NAVAJO NATION

NAVAJO MOUNTAIN

HOPI NATION

SAN FRANCISCO PEAKS

Navajo Nation Map

Naschitti (Nahashch'idí), New Mexico. Courtesy of Lloyd L. Lee.

Introduction

More than 400,000 people are enrolled Navajo Nation citizens, and upward of 150,000 live on the Navajo Nation.[1] The Navajo Nation reservation land base is 27,413 square miles, larger than ten of the fifty states in the United States of America. While the Navajo Treaty of 1868 established an original reservation, Diné people always regard their homeland in relation to their six sacred mountains. This homeland is referred to as Nihikéyah. Nihikéyah means the land the people live and walk upon called home. The Diyin Dine'é (Holy People) created Nihikéyah for the people and instructed them to live within its space. For this book, the term Nihikéyah will be used to refer to Navajo land and the homeland.

Nihikéyah is the world to Diné people. While many Native Nations and communities have been separated from their original homeland through forced removal and live elsewhere, Diné people continue to live on their original homeland, even though some of the land is not designated as part of the federal reservation.

Nihikéyah is more than a commodity and property for the people; it is their foundation and hóózhóǫgo iiná (beauty way of life). Nihikéyah is a physical, emotional, psychological, and spiritual existence for the people. Nihikéyah is the core of what it means to be human and Diné. Nihikéyah's energy and spirit are reflected in the creation scripture, journey narratives, matrix, and way of life.

In this book, the eight contributors are organized following a distinct Navajo matrix and categorized in the cardinal directions, focusing on Nihikéyah's spirit and the challenges the homeland faces, including climate change, oppression, bureaucracy, and the Western legal system. The contributors' examinations, analyses, and/or reflections display a distinct Diné or Navajo matrix. While many non-Diné or non-Navajo have written about the land, philosophy, history, and so many other topics on the Navajo Nation, each of the contributors in this book are Diné, grew up or live on the Navajo Nation, and have observed and/or experienced in their lifetime what they are writing about for the reading audience. Their written words embody Nihikéyah, the love, and the concerns each author has for their homeland.

We start with a general description of a part of the Navajo creation narratives to provide context to Nihikéyah. The stories come from the book *Navajo History, Volume I*, compiled by the Navajo Curriculum Center, edited by Ethelou Yazzie, and published by Rough Rock Press in 1971, and Mike Mitchell's *Origins of the Diné*, published in 2001 by the Navajo Studies and Curriculum Center at the Rough Rock Community School. Other versions of these narratives exist, and each one, including this generalized version, are all accurate. The texts used to discuss the creation narratives have long been thought of by Navajo people and scholars as some of the most reliable sources on Diné baa hane' (Navajo history).

Creation Narratives

In the Diné creation scripture, Áłtsé Hastiin (First Man) and Áłtsé Asdzą́ą́ (First Woman) formed the six sacred mountains with soil from the mountains gathered in the third world. In some stories, it is the fourth world where this takes place, and in other stories, it is the fifth world.

Áłtsé Hastiin and Áłtsé Asdzą́ą́ began in the east and planted Sis Naajiní, the sacred mountain of the east. They placed a blanket of white shell down and sprinkled some of the soil First Man brought from the previous world, and more white shell was placed on top and wrapped. Áłtsé Hastiin and Áłtsé Asdzą́ą́ asked Yoołgai Ashkii (White Bead Boy or Dawn Boy) to live in the mountain.

Tsoodził, mountain of the south, was planted similarly with turquoise. Dootł'izhii At'ééd (Turquoise Girl) was asked to live in the mountain.

Dook'o'oosłííd, mountain of the west, was planted with abalone. Diichiłí Ashkii (Abalone Shell Boy) was asked to live in the mountain.

Dibé Nitsaa, mountain of the north, was planted with obsidian. Bááshzhinii At'ééd (Obsidian Girl) was asked to live in the mountain.

Áłtsé Hastiin and Áłtsé Asdzą́ą́ fastened the mountains to the earth. Sis Naajiní was tied with a bolt of white lightning. They covered the mountain with a blanket of daylight and decorated it with black clouds and male rain. Shash (bear) was sent to guard the doorway for Yoołgai Ashkii.

Tsoodził was fastened with a stone knife. The mountain was covered with a blue cloud and decorated with dark mists and female rain. Tł'iish Tsoh (big snake) was sent to guard the doorway for Dootł'izhii At'ééd.

Dook'o' oosłííd was fastened with a sunbeam. The mountain was covered with a yellow cloud and decorated with black clouds and male rain. Níłch'ih Diłhxił (black wind) was sent to guard the doorway for Diichiłí Ashkii.

Dibé Nitsaa was fastened with a rainbow. The mountain was covered with darkness and decorated with obsidian. Atsiniłtł'ish (lightning) was sent to guard the doorway for Bááshzhinii At'ééd.

Nihikéyah was created, and the Diyin Dine'é also created the first sweat bath, hogan, sun, moon, stars, seasons, and harvest. Along with these creations, the female entities gave birth to monsters. The female entities became pregnant during the separation in the previous world. They placed their babies in meadows, mountains, canyons, on top of rocks, and in some cases in the middle of nowhere. The babies survived, matured, and terrorized the people. The Diyin Dine'é met to discuss how to deal with the monsters. They decided a baby girl would be born to help resolve this problem.

One morning at a sacred place known as Ch'óol'į́'į́ (Gobernador Knob), clouds came and covered the mountain. The clouds were Ádiłhxił (male black cloud), K'os Diłhxił (female black cloud), Níłtsą́ Biką' (male rain), Níłtsą́ Bi'áád (female rain), and Neestiin (mist). Within the clouds, a sacred space was formed. Songs, prayers, and chants were said, and under a rainbow in four days a baby girl was created. In twelve days, the baby girl became a beautiful young woman and started her menstrual cycle. She would be known as White Shell Woman or Changing Woman.

One day Changing Woman was gathering wood before sundown. She sat down on a rock to rest for a while. The wood was all tied in a bundle on her back. When she tried to pick up the bundle to take home, something held the bundle down. She could not stand. She struggled to lift the bundle, and after the fourth attempt, she looked up and saw a young hand-some man standing near her. The man told her to meet him at the water-fall. She went. At the waterfall, the young man impregnated her through his mind. She did not know who this young man was, but later found out it was the Sun Bearer. In time, Changing Woman gave birth. It was a difficult process. She gave birth to twins, Naayéé' Neezghání (Monster Slayer) and Tó Bájíshchíní (Child Born of Water), with the help of the Diyin Dine'é.

Their mother and the Diyin Dine'é loved the twins. The twins played around their home and as they got older asked about their father. Chang-ing Woman did not answer them, sometimes saying that some other person is their father, trying to mislead the twins. She feared Sun Bearer would kill her sons.

One day as the twins were playing close by, the earth started to shake and Changing Woman immediately hid her sons inside their hogan. A gi-ant monster came and demanded to know whose tiny tracks were outside. Changing Woman was able to persuade the monster she made those tiny tracks. He left and the twins came out of hiding. They were not afraid and vowed to kill the giant. They asked their mom constantly about their fa-ther. When she felt they were ready, she told them their father was the Sun Bearer. She described him as powerful and mean. They wanted to visit him to ask for his help to destroy the monsters. The twins said their farewells to their mother and left on the long journey to their father's house. Changing Woman wished her sons well and prayed for their safety.

The twins met several entities on the journey to see their father. Some of the entities they met included Na'ashjé'ii 'Asdzą́ą́ (Spider Woman), Haashch'ééshzhiní (Black God), and Wóóshiyishí (Measuring Worm). The entities told the twins they would face many challenges and tests along their journey. They did face challenges and tests, and they overcame each one.

When they arrived at their father's house, they faced more challenges, which they overcame through the use of sacred names, prayers, chants, and powers. A beautiful woman met them and asked what they wanted. They told her they wanted to see their father, but she knew the Sun Bearer would try to kill them when he returned home. She hid them, and when the Sun Bearer returned home, he asked about the two boys. The wife scolded the Sun Bearer for having children with another entity while he searched the home for them. He eventually found them and tried to kill them immediately. The twins told the Sun Bearer he was their father. He tested them twice, and they remained unharmed. They were allowed to sleep at their father's home. When they woke up, the Sun Bearer tested them twice again, and they were not harmed. Finally, the Sun Bearer conceded the twins were truly his children.

The Sun Bearer finally accepted them as his sons. He offered them many gifts; however, they refused. They instead requested two weapons to help them kill the monsters. The two weapons were 'Atsiniltł'ish K'aa' (Zigzag Lightning Arrow) and 'Atsoolghał K'aa' (Straight Lightning Arrow). Sun Bearer thought about it for some time and decided to give them the weapons, even though some of the monsters were his children. He made a request: when the twins killed Yé'iitsoh T'ááłá'í Naagháii (Big Monster), they were to bring him the headdress. They agreed. The Sun Bearer gave Monster Slayer a zigzag lightning arrow and Child Born of Water a straight lightning arrow. He told them information about Yé'iitsoh, too.

The twins traveled to Tó Sido (Hot Springs) near Tsoodził via a lightning bolt. They waited for Yé'iitsoh, who returned to the lake where they confronted him. Two powerful lightning flashes hit Yé'iitsoh and several flint arrows were shot at him, killing him. They also prevented his blood from coming together and reaching the lake. If it had, he would have been brought back to life. The twins acquired the headdress and gave it to their father as he requested. They cut up Yé'iitsoh's body and placed the parts in different locations around Nihikéyah. They also scalped him and took it home with them. They returned home and told their mother about their feats, meeting their father, and killing Yé'iitsoh. At first, Changing Woman did not believe her sons until they showed her Yé'iitsoh's scalp.

Monster Slayer went out to kill other monsters on his own, and his brother watched him via two wands, K'eet'áán Yáłti'. One was a medicine wand and the other a prayer wand. If Monster Slayer needed help, the wands started to burn brightly. Child Born of Water would smoke the medicine wand and blow smoke on the prayer wand in the four directions and pray for his brother. This was supposed to give Monster Slayer renewed strength to destroy the monster.

Monster Slayer searched for monsters all over the land, and he was able to track down many and kill them. He returned home to rest, and in a short time, he saw red smoke way off into the distance. He went to investigate and found a hole in the ground. In the hole, he saw old men. He learned these old men were sleep, hunger, poverty, lice, and old age. He wanted to kill them all, but the old men were able to persuade Monster Slayer not to kill them because the people would suffer without them. He returned home, where he informed his mother and brother about what he found. He traveled to all corners of Nihikéyah to make sure all the monsters were dead. When no other monsters were located, he returned home.

The twins' work was complete. They laid down their weapons and took off their armor. The twins returned all the armor and weapons to their father, and in return he bestowed gifts. The twins wanted all the gifts their father showed them. He agreed to their request. The people obtained wild animals, domesticated animals, fruits, vegetables, precious stones, rain, wind, snow, and many other things.

The twins returned to their mother and settled down near her home. After a short period, Monster Slayer began to have nightmares and disappeared for days searching for monsters. He saw monsters everywhere he went, and Changing Woman was concerned for her son. The Diyin Dine'é gathered to discuss his condition, and one of them said the spirits of the slain monsters had come back to torment his conscience. A ceremony was created to address the issue, and parts of the Enemy way ceremony (Nidáá') come from this creation. The ceremony worked on the fourth try, and Monster Slayer became well.

The Sun Bearer asked Changing Woman to live with him. He promised to build a beautiful home on an island in the ocean to the west and everything would be provided for her. She did not want to leave Nihikéyah; however, her sons, the Diyin Dine'é, and the Sun Bearer convinced her to move to her new home in the west. Her sons also went with her.

Soon, the Diyin Dine'é met to discuss who would live on Nihikéyah. Changing Woman heard the news and thought humans should inhabit the land. She created humans by rubbing skin from her breast, back, and under both arms. From these first humans, she created the first four clans. The skin from her breast formed the Kinyaa'áanii (Towering House), the skin from her back formed the Honágháahnii (One Who Walks around You), the skin from her right armpit formed the Tódích'íí'nii (Bitter Water), and the skin from her left armpit formed the Hashtł'ishnii (Mud). She gave each group a cane made up of white shell, turquoise, abalone, and jet, and an animal protector of bear, mountain lion, bull snake, and porcupine. Each group was given water, roasted corn, meat jerky, and corn pollen.

With the animal protectors, the four groups left for Nihikéyah. They encountered different entities and peoples along their journey. The animal protectors fought off enemies. The people used their canes to find water at various locations. They walked a long distance and came through various points and reached a place between Ch'óol'í̜'í̜ (Gobernador Knob) and Dził Ná'oodiłii (Huerfano Mountain). The place was named Dinétah (Place of the People) because it was where Changing Woman lived and raised her children. First Man and First Woman also lived in the area. The Diné people were home.

The Diyin Dine'é became very close to the people and visited numerous times. They taught them many cultural teachings. Through these teachings, the people learn to live at home within the six sacred mountains.

Pre–Long Walk Era

Klara Kelley and Harris Francis document the Pre–Long Walk Era of Diné people on Nihikéyah in *A Diné History of Navajoland* (2019). As Kelley and Francis state, the people originated at Hajíínáí (Emergence place) and interacted with the Kiis'áanii (villagers, including pre-Columbian Anaasází). The two groups traded and intermarried. The interactions between Diné and Kiis'áanii and eventually with other groups of people show a long connection the people have with Nihikéyah.

The Diné people lived in extended family networks. They grew crops like corn and hunted game such as deer and antelope in the mountains. They learned to sustain their foods, ceremonies, ways, and language for generations with the land and continue to do so into the twenty-first century. Ceremonial oral tradition and narratives tell of Nihikéyah based on verbal maps; however, not all Diné people have knowledge and access to the verbal maps. Ceremonial knowledge keepers share with apprentices or trusted family members only. The verbal maps are not for everyone and are protected from outsiders. Kelley and Francis discuss verbal maps in *A Diné History of Navajoland* (2019); however, they do not reveal any new narratives not already documented. The verbal maps are designed to be protected.

Diné people's relationship with Nihikéyah and other human beings in the region reflects family, care, responsibility, love, and respect. Diné clans also show their relationship with the homeland. Many of the clans today have a connection to the land and to the nihizází (our ancestors). The nihizází extended across all over Nihikéyah. In *A Diné History of Navajoland*, Kelley and Francis discuss the clan histories, relations with other Indigenous peoples in the region, and the concept of ethnogenesis. These histories show the bond between many peoples and the land.

In the Diné extended family network system, every few years, a large gathering called a naachid was called. This gathering brought together large extended family networks, peace leaders, and war leaders to discuss pertinent issues impacting the families or areas, including conflicts with other Indigenous peoples, drought, or something requiring discussion and a vital decision. Ceremonies such as a hózhóójí (blessing way) were conducted. The gatherings sometimes took a month or a season. Depending on what was discussed, the peace leaders conducted the gathering or the war leaders led.

The people interacted with many Indigenous peoples such as the Comanches, Kiowas, Utes, Paiutes, Havasupai, Hopi, Apache, and Pueblos. The people did not have a centralized governing system and a central leader; rather, the extended family networks governed. Among these networks, it was common to see various leaders, including a medicine healer and matriarch (usually a great-grandmother).

The people established trading network systems stretching for hundreds of miles in all four directions. A distinctive way of life and a strong community were established. Certain locations on the homeland grew corn and beans. The people were very knowledgeable about the homeland and had deep reciprocal relations.

Beginning in the sixteenth and continuing into the nineteenth century, Spanish and Mexican peoples invaded the homeland and interacted with all Native peoples in the Southwest. Their ways influenced the Diné people and Native peoples in the region. A significant impact was the introduction of livestock—sheep, goats, cows, and horses. It is important to note, according to the creation scripture, the Sun Bearer introduced sheep and livestock to the people when his sons, the twin protectors, brought them back to the people.

Besides taking care of the sheep and learning how to use the horse effectively, warfare jolted the people. Spanish, Mexican, New Mexican, and American military conflicts occurred from 1540 to 1868. Diné people defended themselves. The conflicts resulted in the capture and/or death of

Diné men, women, and children. The conflicts usually were attempts by family members or relatives to rescue loved ones.

Diné people adapted to the changing situations to ensure their survival. They worked together and moved around Nihikéyah. They helped one another to secure the safest locations and homes. Traumatic changes took place with the American invasion and the people's internment at Bosque Redondo.

Post–Long Walk/Reservation Era

From 1846 to 1864, conflicts between the American military and the Diné people were frequent. Several treaties were signed to make peace; however, all were broken. Most Diné people kept to themselves and did not raid Pueblo and New Mexican settlements, although a few Diné individuals did so.

In the summer of 1863, U.S. Army General James Carleton ordered Lieutenant Colonel Christopher "Kit" Carson to "round up" the Diné people. Carson employed Utes, various Pueblos, Hopis, and the Diné Anaa'í (enemy of the people) to help in his campaign. By the winter of 1863–1864, hundreds of Diné people surrendered to Carson. Carson carried out a scorched earth policy to subdue and subjugate the people. From 1864 to 1866, Carson and the U.S. military "rounded up" thousands of Diné men, women, and children, and forced them to march over three hundred miles to the Bosque Redondo prison camp, where hundreds of Mescalero Apache people were interned as well, near present-day Fort Sumner, New Mexico. From 1864 to 1866, fifty-three forced marches and ten thousand Diné people were removed to Bosque Redondo. While thousands were at Fort Sumner, hundreds eluded capture and hid in the Grand Canyon, the Naatsis'áán (Navajo Mountain) region, or among various Pueblo villages with relatives. They maintained their way of life, while at the same time remaining watchful for the possibility of an American attack.

Diné people suffered tremendously at Bosque Redondo. Diné people refer to Bosque Redondo as hwéeldi, which means "people suffering." The land at Bosque Redondo could not sustain corn because the nearby Pecos River was salty. The people depended on government food rations; the food was so different it made them weak and sick, and some died from it. In addition, the Comanches and New Mexican settlers raided

the camp and snatched women and children to sell as slaves. Diseases
ravaged the camp, and many people died during the incarceration.[2] Even
with the enormous suffering, Diné hataałii (healers) prayed to keep everyone strong and hopeful. All Diné people wanted desperately to return
to Nihikéyah.

The Diné leadership at the time did not want their families to suffer
anymore and constantly implored the American military to allow them
to return home. Barboncito, Manuelito, Armijo, Delgado, Herrero, Chi-
queto, Muerto de Hombre, Hombro, Narbano, Narbono Segundo, Ganado
Mucho, and Largo (all Spanish surnames of Navajo leaders) purposefully
negotiated with the U.S. government to return home.

In the spring of 1868, the federal government sent General William T.
Sherman and Colonel Samuel F. Tappan to negotiate a treaty with Diné
people. A treaty was signed on June 1, 1868, allowing the people to return
to Nihikéyah. The treaty stipulated the people would no longer "raid,"
and they would stay within the reservation boundaries established by the
American government.[3] The reservation boundaries were the following:

> Bounded on the north by the 37th degree of north latitude, south by an
> east and west line passing through the site of old Fort Defiance, in Canon
> Bonito, east by the parallel of longitude which, if prolonged south, would
> pass through old Fort Lyon, or the Ojo-de-oso, Bear Spring, and west by
> the parallel of longitude about 109'30' west of Greenwich, provided it em-
> braces the outlet of the Canon-de-Chilly, which canon is to be all included
> in this reservation, shall be, and the same is hereby, set apart for the use and
> occupation of the Navajo tribe of Indians.[4]

The treaty also stipulated the people could not oppose the building of
railroad lines through their homeland, and they were required to send
their children to government schools. The federal government in return
provided seeds, farm equipment, and livestock.

The people left Bosque Redondo on June 18, 1868. More than 7,300 people walked the 35 days to reach Fort Wingate, New Mexico. They stayed at
Fort Wingate until January 1869. Livestock was not distributed until November 1869. Each man, woman, and child received two animals. Barboncito, one of the leaders who signed the treaty, spoke of the importance of
the livestock: "Now you are beginning again. Take care of the sheep that
have been given to you, as you care for your own children. Never kill them

for food. If you are hungry, go out after the wild animals and the wild plants. Or go without food, for you have done that before. These few sheep must grow into flocks so that we, the people, can be as we once were."[5]

The impact of hwéeldi was life-altering. The people began to see themselves as one large community. New traditions developed, men learned new trades, women started to use American/commercial yarn for weaving, and the people were exposed to American and Christian thought, ways, values, and attitudes. Returning to Nihikéyah helped the people grow and prosper for the next seventy-plus years from 1869 to 1945.

The people returned to where they had been living prior to hwéeldi. No signposts or fences existed, and the government did not force the people to live within the stated reservation boundaries. Within ten years, President Rutherford B. Hayes signed an executive order pushing the reservation boundary twenty miles to the west because Diné leadership lobbied the federal government to increase the reservation boundaries. For the next sixty years, lands were added to the reservation via presidential executive orders and congressional confirmation. Most of the additional lands occurred on the western part of the reservation in Arizona territory. Allotments and opposition from the New Mexico congressional delegation and a few past Navajo leaders such as Jacob Morgan fenced in the eastern part of the reservation. Morgan did not want more grazing lands because he wanted the people to assimilate to an American way of life where sheep herding and ranching was in the past. The eastern part of the reservation developed into a patchwork of reservation and non-reservation land, known as the checkerboard area. Additional lands in Arizona and southeastern Utah were designated as part of the Navajo reservation in the early twentieth century.

Challenges for Nihikéyah

The people experienced a monumental transition from the end of World War II in 1945 through the 1990s. Education, health care, economic development, voting rights, religious freedom, mineral extraction, and the changing economy impacted Diné people's way of life. More people began to work in the wage labor system, and children were sent to schools created to assimilate Diné youth and to remove them from their families, communities, and Nihikéyah. Western education became the foremost priority for Diné people; however, the impact of American education from public, boarding, parochial, and special vocational programs changed younger Navajo generations. Diné bizaad was prohibited, and many families encouraged their children to learn to speak English. Along with an American education, more people left the reservation to get away from problems and the "backward" way of life. They sought economic and educational opportunities.

The Navajo tribal council sought ways to develop the reservation economy, such as allowing mining on Nihikéyah. In many cases, council decisions were done for the betterment of communities; nonetheless, the results negatively affected the people and homeland. For example, Kerr-McGee and Vanadium Corporation of America established uranium mines on the reservation in the 1950s.[6] The companies never told the people or the council the dangers of working in uranium mines. From 1952 to 1963, hundreds of Diné men worked for Kerr-McGee in the uranium mines near Shiprock, New Mexico.[7] Scores of Navajo men and women died later from lung cancer.[8] Other mineral extraction projects were approved by the council in the 1960s, such as Peabody Coal Company mining on Black Mesa. The approval of Peabody Coal Company to mine Black Mesa and to use precious underground water to transport the coal to the Mohave generating power plant in Nevada forced the removal of many Diné families from their homes, as well as some Hopi families from the 1970s to the 2000s.

Along with mineral extraction development on Nihikéyah, overgrazing was a concern. The federal government told Diné people to reduce their livestock, which the people strongly opposed. The people were never consulted about overgrazing. The federal government implemented livestock reduction in the 1930s and 1940s. Many families lost their self-sufficiency and left the reservation to find work in border towns and cities such as Gallup, Farmington, Winslow, Holbrook, Flagstaff, Phoenix, and Albuquerque.

Industrial development on the land became a central fixture for the Navajo economy in the late 1940s and 1950s. It did provide some positive aspects yet the negative consequences to the homeland and people such as lack of sanitation, clean and safe water, utilities, and housing was evident. Tourism became more prominent especially when Hollywood director and producer John Ford filmed seven movies in Monument Valley from 1939 to 1960. The John Ford films created international interest in the Navajo Nation. It brought thousands of tourists who wanted to see John Wayne and "Indians." It helped create some infrastructure, such as paved roads and the first Navajo tribal park at Monument Valley in 1960.

Large parcels of lands were added to the original reservation because of the people living in the same areas prior to Bosque Redondo, the high number of livestock grazing the lands, and through effective Congressional lobbying by Navajo leaders such as Chee Dodge. From the late 1870s through the 1930s, U.S. presidents Rutherford B. Hayes, Chester A. Arthur, Grover Cleveland, William McKinley, Theodore Roosevelt, Woodrow Wilson, Herbert Hoover, and Franklin D. Roosevelt issued executive orders adding lands to the original Navajo reservation. Eventually, Congress put a stop to this when they passed a law proposed by Arizona Representative Marcus Aurelius Smith, who opposed adding more land to the Navajo Nation in the state of Arizona. From this point forward, the Navajo Nation needed to protect what they had and be on guard for the possibility of Nihikéyah being taken from the people.

With these constant challenges, the people, council delegates, and allies worked hard to ensure Nihikéyah was protected from outside intervention. In the twenty-first century, Diné people are still confronted with many similar challenges including environmental protection, economic development, education, health care, public safety, homesite leasing, and other relevant matters. Nihikéyah is vital to and sacred for the people, yet threats exist. The threats need to be repelled, and the Navajo Nation should advocate for a paradigm shift where acknowledging, respecting, and sustaining Nihikéyah is the primary objective.

The Focus of This Book

Nihikéyah is a hallowed place and home for Diné people. The Diyin Dine'é created this homeland and instructed the people to live here because it was specifically made for them. More than 400,000 Diné people are attached to the land, and up to 150,000 live on the Navajo Nation in the twenty-first century, while many others live in close proximity in neighboring cities and towns.

The homeland is the foundation of the people and integral to the people's existence and way of life. The people worked hard to sustain their original land base, even though some of the original land is no longer acknowledged by the federal government as part of the current reservation.

Nihikéyah is more than property or a commodity to the people. It is their existence. The land is a physical, emotional, psychological, and spiritual world. It has energy and spirit supplying the necessary support and love for the people.

This book and the contributors prove the vitality of the homeland, consider the challenges the land faces, and propose methods of defending the land from all kinds of monsters. The book is organized based on the Navajo philosophy of learning T'áá Diné Bo'óhoo'aah Bindii'a'. This philosophy of learning's orientation follows a sunwise pattern and provides meaning to a person's life cycle, parts of the day, seasons, knowledge process, and the sacred mountains, which are attached to each direction. The eastern direction represents birth, dawn, spring, thinking, and the sacred mountain Sis Naajiní (Blanca Peak in Colorado). The southern direction represents adolescence, day, summer, planning, and the sacred mountain Tsoodził (Mount Taylor in New Mexico). The western direction represents adulthood, evening, fall, living, and the sacred mountain Dook'oosłííd (San Francisco Peaks in Arizona). The northern direction represents old age, night, winter, reflection, and the sacred mountain Dibé Nitsaa (Mount Hersperus in Colorado).

Each contributor is placed in a cardinal direction based on their rearing and/or present living location. Each of these contributors grew up or live in one of the identified directions/locations. The chapters also reflect the knowledge process of thinking, planning, living, and reflecting. While the chapters are categorized by the cardinal directions, the reader will notice the shared and common theme of sustaining a Diné way of life and how the land is an integral element. In other words, all the chapters are interwoven together to present a distinct Diné matrix in the twenty-first century with Nihikéyah as the foundation.

We start in the east, symbolizing birth, dawn, spring, and thinking (nitsáhákees). The two contributors are Jonathan Perry and Mario Atencio. Jonathan Perry's chapter "Ha'a'aahdę́ę́' Ntsékees: Concepts of Land from an Eastern Navajo Leader" examines Diné fundamental law, eastern Navajo lands, challenges, and the importance of sustaining cultural teachings. His chapter starts off with what individual Diné see in the land, the meaning of the land to each person and their community, and the relation, reflection, and drive to sustaining and protecting the land. The second chapter by Mario Atencio, titled "Dinétahdi Kéédahwiiniit'įįgi Ayóo Dahnihidziil," is short yet critical. Atencio discusses defending Nihikéyah from the pollution monsters, including the American government, oil and gas companies, state governments, and institutions working to contaminate Nihikéyah. Atencio advocates for a new paradigm shift and methods to protect Nihikéyah. The land, air, water, and sacred places will tell the people how this will be done.

Next, we follow the sunwise motion to the south, symbolizing adolescence, day, summer, and planning (nahat'á). The two authors of this section are Jake Skeets and Manny Loley. Jake Skeets's chapter, titled "Form, Memory: Mapping Land Through Diné Poetry," is an alluring work interweaving Diné language (Diné bizaad), land, memory, and mapping to human existence. Skeets presents readers with some thoughts on what these concepts are for a Diné person and how a human being comprehends life and feels a link to the land. The fourth chapter by Manny Loley, titled "My Breath Is Rain Essence: Ruminations on Rain, Land, Language, Time, and Storytelling in Diné Thought," focuses on rain, land, language, time, and storytelling. The chapter does a stimulating job of bringing to the forefront a twenty-first century Diné paradigm and how one person translates it to living in Nihikéyah. Loley presents the reader with the interlacing of the land with the fundamentals of rain, language, time, and storytelling. This fusion displays how a Diné matrix is different from American thought in the sense that land is in relation with all living entities on the earth and is part of the family not separate or independent.

Third, we move to the west, representing adulthood, evening, fall, and living (iiná). The two authors are Shawn Attakai and Wendy S. Greyeyes. In chapter 5, Shawn Attakai's "Challenges to Diné Bikéyah in 2023: Nihikéyah Bich'ą́ą́h Yéiilti' Doo" examines Diné understandings of the homeland, challenges the Diné people and land face, and how the people can address the challenges particularly oppression and injustice. In chapter 6, Wendy S. Greyeyes's "Rethinking Nihikéyah Consciousness: Defying Lateral Animosities and Bureaucratic Mazes of Homesite Lease Living" is a compelling narration of the Navajo Nation homesite leasing process. The process is bureaucratic, American, and does not allow for a Diné-centric approach. She advocates for a new consciousness based on Diné values. Her personal experience through the homesite leasing process is not dissimilar to every Diné person who attempts to acquire a homesite lease yet shows the need to develop a process where Diné values are primary. She also proposes a transformative land reform policy.

For the final section, we move to the north, representing old age, night, winter, and reflecting (siihasin). The two authors of this section are Rex

Lee Jim and Jennifer Jackson Wheeler. Chapter 7, Rex Lee Jim's "The Footprints We Leave: Claiming Stewardship over Diné Bikéyah," intertwines cultural knowledge with the land he walks upon. Skeets and Loley provide a similar perspective; however, Jim shows how cultural knowledge and land are one in the same and how the people lived with the land not separated or disconnected. In chapter 8, Jennifer Jackson Wheeler's "On the Land That Holds My Birth Cord" is a creative fiction piece on how one family loves all of its relatives, including Nihikéyah. For Diné people, the land is a part of the family, and the people's experiences on the land display how the land is not thought of as a separate lifeless entity; rather, the land is a relative for Diné families. The creative fiction piece is based on Wheeler's real-life experiences and reflects a Diné existential way of being.

While this book is not an exhaustive examination into Nihikéyah, it does bring to the forefront the meaning of the homeland for and by the Diné people and the challenges the people must confront and overcome. The book is part of the ongoing campaign to sustain hózhóǫgo iiná and Nihikéyah for the many generations to come.

Notes

1.   U.S. Bureau of the Census, *The American Indian and Alaska Native Population: 2010, 2010 Census Briefs*, prepared by the U.S. Department of Commerce Economics and Statistics Administration, Bureau of the Census, Washington, D.C., 2012.
2.   New Mexico Department of Cultural Affairs, "The Story of Bosque Redondo," 2005.
3.   "Treaty Between the United States of America and the Navajo Tribe of Indians," July 25, 1868.
4.   "Treaty Between the United States of America and the Navajo Tribe of Indians," July 25, 1868.
5.   New Mexico Department of Cultural Affairs, "The Story of Bosque Redondo," 2005.
6.   Donald A. Grinde and Bruce E. Johansen, *Ecocide of Native America: Environmental Destruction of Indian Lands and Peoples* (Santa Fe, N.M.: Clear Light Publishers, 1995); Peter Iverson and Monty Roessel, *Diné: A History of the Navajos* (Albuquerque: University of New Mexico Press, 2002), 219; Navajo Uranium Workers Oral History Project, Doug Brugge, coordinator, PIPC.
7.   Iverson and Roessel, *Diné: A History of the Navajos*, 219.
8.   Grinde and Johansen, *Ecocide of Native America*, 208–209; Iverson and Roessel, *Diné: A History of the Navajos*, 219.

HA'A'AAH / EAST

Melons in the garden. Courtesy of Lloyd L. Lee.

CHAPTER 1

Ha'a'aahdę́ę́' Ntsékees

Concepts of Land from an Eastern Navajo Leader

JONATHAN PERRY

Introduction

It is hard not to reflect on myself and my cultural teachings as I look over the landscape in my home region of the Navajo Nation. When I scan the horizon and see the world around me, I can't help but feel at home on the land that many generations of my family lived on before me. I appreciate how I am connected to my homeland. Diné cultural teachings have always been a part of my foundation that I continue to carry with me throughout my life. I am happy to share my reflections of my journey so far and what the land means to me. What I provide is from my understanding of the teachings given to me by elders in my community and family. There may be variations of concepts from region to region. My thoughts being shared are also based on my experience and not so much from academia.

I believe my path was made for me long before I realized by many people in my home community of Becenti, New Mexico. I grew up in an area that is known by several traditional Diné names in the Eastern Navajo region. My community has two common Navajo names, which are Tł'óó'di Tsin, which translates to Remote Forest, and Jádi Háádi T'ííh, which translates to Antelope Lookout. These areas are my foundation, as my roots have been planted through many generations of family who lived in the community. This is the beginning of my teachings as part of identifying who I am and my place within the universe around us.

I am regarded as a Naat'áanii among many Diné across the Navajo Nation, specifically across the Eastern Navajo region. This is because I have

dedicated my life toward working for my Diné people. I have served as
a volunteer in many community-based organizations that work to protect Navajo homelands, natural resources, and cultural areas. I have also
served in several political positions within the Navajo Nation government
that include Navajo Nation Council Delegate, Becenti Chapter President,
Becenti Chapter Vice President, and Commissioner on the Eastern Navajo Land Commission. Often, I'm also requested to provide guidance
to committees at the Navajo chapter governance level regarding land use
planning, preservation of local historical areas, and incorporating Diné
values and principles into policies and procedures.

The role of being a leader among Diné is sacred, and there is much responsibility. I am humbled by the many years that I have been allowed to
speak and represent interests on behalf of my people. During my journey
on the leadership path, I have acquired more knowledge in traditional
Diné concepts that have influenced my stance on many topics and issues
on the Navajo Nation. There is a constant cycle of learning and developing as more traditional education is provided through experience in
community work and advanced understanding of Diné ceremonies and
philosophy.

My first teaching as I was growing up was learning to identify myself
and knowing my place in this world. I was surrounded by maternal relatives as a child, and I was taught the importance of women in our families
and community; this is evident with the Navajo Nation being a matriarchal
society. My mother, my aunts, and my maternal grandmother were key
teachers who provided me with lasting cultural knowledge that I still use
today. Speaking and understanding Diné Bizáád, the Navajo language, has
always been important in my home as I was growing by elders in my family
and I appreciate their values in preserving our sacred language. Today I am
able to continue to communicate in Diné Bizáád.

My mother continued the tradition of burying my umbilical cord in
the area my maternal family is rooted in. That practice is important to the
Diné people, as it creates the bond of a child to their homeland and will
serve as the permanent connection of that individual to their homeland.
As I was developing as a teenager, I was shared information on different
areas where ceremonies were held, where medicinal herbs were located,
and where historical events took place. I was told by elders in my family
that those sacred areas help identify new generations of people to their

ancestors and the locations where they lived and protected. The ability to connect different areas across my homeland to my family history helped create the understanding of the value of the land to my own identity.

When I was younger, I did not know that I would take the leadership path in life, but I now look back and appreciate what I was taught. Today I have the passion to protect our homelands and look at the land in a way that is unique to the Diné people. I am able to understand how the Navajo culture provides traditional concepts of governance as it relates to Diné Bibee Haz'áanii, or Diné Fundamental Law. The traditional concepts that I'm speaking of are revealed through ceremonial songs and stories, prayers, and clan stories.

Before going into more details on the components of Diné Fundamental Law, it seems important to discuss the philosophy of k'éh. Often the teachings of k'éh are simply shared as the relationship between an individual with other members of their family and community based on their four clans. But there are more complex teachings that go further for an individual to identify themselves and their relationship with all life around them. This in-depth concept of k'éh teaches Navajo people that they are not only Diné, but through their divine responsibility of ceremonies, their identity is Nahokáá' Diyin Dine'é or Holy Surface People.

Nahokáá' Diyin Dine'é have been given the responsibility of traditional ceremonies that are important in maintaining hózhǫ́, the balance of harmony. K'éh at this level of knowledge is given to individuals to know their relationship to Nihimá Nahasdzáán, our Mother Earth, and Yádiłhił Nihitaa', our Father Sky. This is how we acknowledge our relatives at a universal level and that we see all forms of life with respect. Diyin Dine'é, or Holy People, identify and relate to Nahookáá' Diyin Dine'é through traditional Navajo names, clanship, traditional clothing and jewelry, and original Diné language. Individuals are also taught through ceremony and prayers that the place given for the Nahookáá' Diyin Dine'é is among the sacred mountains of Sis Naajiní or Blanca Peak, Tsoodził or Mount Taylor, Dook'o'oosłííd or the San Francisco Peaks, Dibé Nitsaa or Mount Hesperus, Dził Ná'oodiłii or Huerfano Mountain, and Dził Ch'óól'į́'į́ or Gobernador Knob.

The Diné clanship system is important when we view land because of the history of clans in certain regions. There are many sites across the Navajo homelands that are connected to many of the Diné clans. The same can be said with animals that are native to the different regions of Navajo lands, which are connected with clans. Some examples include Kin-yaa'áanii, or Towering House Clan, with the bear; Tó dích'íí'nii, or Bitter Water Clan, with the wolf; Hónághááhnii, or One Who Walks Around Clan, with the mountain lion; and Hashtł'ishnii, or Mud People Clan, with the porcupine. These teachings can vary from region to region on the Navajo Nation and are rooted in Diné customary law.

In Diné ceremonies, land is important along with the different herbs used that are collected from different areas on the Navajo Nation and other traditional areas to the Diné. The jish or medicine bundle has sacred items collected from sacred areas and mountains, important herbs, and buckskin that have been obtained in the traditional Diné way, with no use of bullets or knives. When ceremonies are conducted, the patient, their family, and the medicine people assisting all come together and share their clans to establish their relationship for a sacred connection. The traditional Navajo names are used in ceremonies and aren't shared openly as the names identify people to the Diyin Dine'é who are called upon during different healing ceremonies. This is another important connection to the land that Diné people have throughout their lifetime.

As I share my reflection, it is important for our Diné people to seek traditional knowledge through their elders and the medicine people from their regions, as there are variations to the information. It can be complicated to bring this type of knowledge forward, as much of this is not found in books and other printed reference material but only in ceremony within the hooghan or traditional homes of the Diné.

Diné Concepts on Land

I look at Diné Fundamental Law as the primary framework to establish my concepts on the land. Diné Fundamental Law has been in existence among the Navajo for time immemorial. The principles of those laws have never changed but have been able to provide direction and a good balance of hózhǫ́ for many generations. There are four primary parts to Diné Fundamental Law that include traditional law, customary law, natural law, and common law. The four primary components cover different aspects of Diné life. It begins with an individual as a child of the Diyin Dine'é. Then it extends to family and community along with the world around them. The knowledge of the four directions is embedded in Diné Fundamental Law with nitsáhákees, or thinking, to the east; nahat'á, or planning, to the south; iiná, or life, to the west; and siihasin, or hope and reflection, to the north.

With the understanding of Diné Fundamental Law and K'éh, we acknowledge and respect our Mother Earth, which is the land. We should know the placement of the mountains and the elements within the earth have purpose as they were set in their locations by the Diyin Dine'é with the intention of protecting and preserving the livelihood of the Diné people. The rivers, lakes, and aquifers provide us with water that helps us to sustain our lives, our livestock, wildlife, and vegetation including medicinal herbs. It is important to defend areas and natural elements that sustain life because once we lose those sacred gifts from the Diyin Dine'é, we will not last long.

In traditional Navajo stories, we are told that the Diné had to travel through previous worlds before coming to this one we live in now. With each world the Diné passed through, they were given more tools, ceremonies, and knowledge so that they will live in hózhǫ́. In addition to that, the Diné people also acknowledged different animals and life-forms that help guide the people into this world. This teaching shows that clans, areas across the land, and ceremonies are inclusive of animals. Diné natural law brings in this aspect of traditional teachings, as it provides information on the people's relationship to the animals and the natural world.

In this world it is important for us to maintain the value of the natural world and preserve all significant areas important to our identity and our ceremonies. That is what makes us Diné, along with our language. We are told that we are stewards of our homelands and it is our responsibility to care for what the Diyin Dine'é provided us for the safety of our livelihood. Once we abuse and exploit our natural world, we will see unbalance and threats to our people from our Mother Earth because she will try to heal herself with every extractive wound we inflict. Every time we damage the earth we violate natural law and cause more disruption that can cause long-term disharmony to our people today and into the future.

The right of Diné to live and establish families is acknowledged in customary law of the Diné. The land provides us with space for a home, gardens, and farms to sustain life. This leads our people to be self-sustaining and promote self-governance. Families are able to provide local leadership among their relatives and seek ceremonies for balance if local relatives violate Diné Fundamental Law. This was seen throughout the history of the Navajo people, as there was no central or unified government structure in traditional Navajo culture. Today the Navajo Nation government is in need of restructuring to align more with Diné cultural values, as outlined in Diné traditional law.

As I work for my people, I often reflect on the need to continue to share knowledge but I have to do so in a respectful manner. This is done by sharing stories only in the winter months and sharing prayers and songs specifically during ceremonies that are allowed in certain seasons. The use of traditional hooghan and táchééh, or sweat lodge, is also crucial as they have spiritual representation in how they are constructed and the space within them. This is why I urge our people to seek out knowledge from Diné elders and medicine people, as they will go more in depth in sacred spaces that are more appropriate.

It takes time to learn from the stories and learn to incorporate the lessons into public work and public policy. An elder I knew years ago would always say we have to think Diné. I interpret that as looking at all issues and work with the base of Diné Fundamental Law and cultural values outlined in our ceremonies. We don't see this in the federal and state governments because according to their views there is a separation of church and state. In Diné concepts, our ceremonies, songs, and prayers are our form of self-governance. This conflicts with how the Navajo Nation government was established. Perhaps this is why the Navajo Nation government doesn't reflect Diné people; the crucial component of Diné Fundamental Law is missing as it was originally created.

For more information on this, I'd refer to the fact that the original Navajo Business Council that was established in 1923 was developed with the intention of addressing oil extraction and approving leases. The Bureau of Indian Affairs never had the intention of incorporating true Diné values in the government structure they imposed. In 1927 when chapter governments were introduced, it was based on districts created by the Bureau of Indian Affairs. That action divided natural communities and traditional local governance structures that were established by Diné Fundamental Law. Today these same structures are still used, and it hasn't allowed for Navajo communities to flourish.

Challenges and Threats

Like many other people of the Navajo Nation, I grew up in an area that was exploited for natural resources in the past. My community was exposed to contamination caused from past uranium mining and milling projects that impacted the land, air, and water. This has caused a majority of my work to focus around uranium mining activities. I have worked to address remediation of radioactive areas on and near the Navajo Nation and prevent new uranium mining projects. Going forward into the future, I will continue to work on this because this is a major injustice that was done to my people and my homeland.

The Navajo Nation has been a target for resource extraction for centuries beginning from the intrusion of European settlers seeking gold and silver. Recent history showed more extractive projects for oil and natural gas, coal, helium, hydrogen, and uranium. These projects have left a legacy of contamination and dangerous abandoned sites across the Navajo Nation. The extractive industry has also left contamination of groundwater, lakes, and rivers that will never be cleaned up to standards that are safe to consume. There are also areas of poor air quality due to coal power plants and flares from oil and natural gas extractive sites. These are examples of violations of Diné natural laws due to the disruption of the natural placement of natural resources. This has caused environmental damages, public health impacts, and other social-economic issues.

I look around me every day and I think of the damage corporations have caused looking for uranium ore. I think of the cost that can never be measured financially, as it is beyond what we can ever afford. I often ask several questions such as the following: How can we put a price on our homeland? Can we put a price tag on our livelihood and health? Why would we put future generations in jeopardy with their health? How do we begin to repair and heal from legacy mines?

For me, uranium mining activities and lasting contamination are examples of a violation of Diné natural law and shortcomings on addressing it without proper use of Diné Fundamental Law. There are hundreds of contaminated sites across the Navajo Nation with no adequate plans for cleanup. Discussions are led by outside federal agencies with plans developed that aren't centered in Diné cultural values. This has caused more issues in Navajo communities and citizens because these plans don't reflect the people or the culture.

Uranium ore has its place deep underground, and naturally placed uranium ore doesn't contaminate as it is not active. Uranium becomes active once it is disturbed and will remain active for billions of years. During the period between the early 1940s to the 1980s, uranium was extracted and processed on traditional Navajo homelands for nuclear weapons and energy. This caused disruption in the natural world, which brought contamination to groundwater, the soil, and air near mining and milling sites. People, animals, and vegetation were exposed to contamination that resulted in destruction and death. Health and environmental impacts affected many life-forms that also impacted Diné culture. Animals that Diné used for food were dangerous to consume. Various herbal vegetation used in different ceremonies stopped growing. Families were broken due to illness and death. Homes and clustered family residences were abandoned due to radioactive exposure. Uranium caused disharmony and broke the balance set forth by Diné Fundamental Law, and this continues to be felt decades after the last uranium mine closed on the Navajo Nation.

Today there is resentment against the nuclear industry because of the past experiences that the Diné people faced. The Diné people acknowledge that no further uranium mining activities should occur on Navajo homelands, but there is constant threat from non-Navajo companies wanting to further exploit natural resources.

There are references to Diné Fundamental Law in policies developed by the Navajo Nation government but the lack of cultural values as the basis for addressing the impacts continues to be missing. Inclusion of impacted communities and medicine people continue to be overlooked by policymakers who do not uphold the traditional use of Naabik'íyáti', or talking it over. Bringing the medicine people and community people together is important to resolving issues through traditional Navajo consensus while respecting Diné Fundamental Law.

As a naat'áanii, I continue to speak on behalf of those who are too young to speak up. I also speak for those who are too tired and those who are in pain from sharing their experiences. I speak for the respect of each individual and their value that the Diyin Dine'é bestowed in them. I do what I can to guide discussions toward healing and addressing current conditions that plague our homelands. I feel there is no need to discuss new projects that can cause more damage to our land and our communities. I also do what I can to be inclusive of everyone who can bring solutions to discussions on healing our homeland from contamination.

Through more education in traditional teachings, we can see that more of our young people will see how crucial Diné values are to bringing hózhǫ́ back to our homelands. Sharing ceremonial knowledge on historical teachings will carry the Diné people into the future. Looking at challenges faced by the communities and our land, uranium is one of many major issues facing the Navajo Nation.

In the different roles that I have worked in over the years, I have also seen other challenges that the Diné people face. I believe that it's also important to highlight some other issues. These challenges can be seen in different areas of the Navajo Nation, just as much as it can be seen in the Eastern Navajo region. In evaluating our existence and our place in the twenty-first century, we have to take note of what negative forces exist. In Diné culture there are stories that many monsters were killed, but there are also monsters that still exist. There are also threats that exist due to the actions and inactions of people.

Another major threat that continues to be present is the concept that land is only seen as property and a commodity only to serve civilization. There is a cycle that exists in the world that includes damaging or contaminating areas of land, then moving on to another area and doing more damage for financial gain. That thought has served the pathway for settlement across the world that only resulted in sacrificing our world for short-term profits. The cycle includes false solutions of isolating those damaged areas and not remediating or revitalizing those lands to predamaged conditions as previously shared.

As long as ownership of land and using plants, animals, sacred elements, and minerals for monetary gain are present, we will always see other lifeforms in the natural world as inferior. If we continue to see everything as commodity, we will never see the true value of the natural world we are part of. The land we live on will always be here after each generation goes; the land is permanent and will continue to provide space for life, if we allow. But people are here for a temporary amount of time, as shared in Diné natural law. It is important to acknowledge that although humans are present for a limited amount of time, their decisions and actions will have long-term affects to the world.

Lack of understanding and maintenance of livestock and other domesticated animals continue to cause disruption to the area ecosystems. For several generations we have seen different impacts to our society and our environment due to overgrazing. The Diné have incorporated livestock such as horses, cattle, sheep, chickens, pigs, and other animals. Many of these animals have sustained the livelihood of many families, and many have practiced proper management. But there is a growing issue of negligence and overgrazing of livestock; this is proving to be an ongoing issue that will have long-term impacts. As overgrazing affects vegetation, water tables, and other natural ecosystems, the long-term affect will be a problem for numerous generations.

Diné have been successful in surviving many hardships and policies focused on elimination and assimilation through the ability of adapting to the ever-changing world and society. As I continue to say today, our Diné people have the ability to make initiatives to take action on plans and policies based on Diné Fundamental Law. The Diné can make necessary movement to address issues that are impacting our homelands. The Navajo Nation has the opportunity to implement better public policy rooted in Diné culture and focused in preservation of the environment and natural resources.

Evidence exists of disruption of the natural world and abuse of natural laws through extensive drought as a result of limited rain, vegetation, and restriction of wildlife habitat. As humans we have the responsibility of maintaining the ecosystem so that it rejuvenates naturally so that there is constantly life that exists in cycles. Whether people are hunting, farming, irrigating, ranching; creating necessities of life such as homes, clothing, blankets, and tools; or developing jewelry or a commodity of value that would promote commerce and bartering, there was a balance of replacing what was disturbed or taken. Diné Fundamental Law also promotes the key notion that every living being and energy has a place and that all identities need to be respected.

As it has been stated before, there is always a process for Diné to bring back balance and harmony to themselves and the world around them. This has yet to happen at a tribal government level. There are little to no plans to bring remediation and correct the wrongs of the past; only when the Diné make a solid action to bring correction can healing really occur. This will take much more than what the Diné have taken, but it will require holding foreigners accountable for their actions against the Diné and the land due to exploitation. This will also require the Diné to abandon the foreign model of governance that was imposed and reintroduce a more culturally traditional form of governance for the Diné people.

Looking Forward

Another important role of being considered a naat'áanii is guiding others back onto a path that heals any damages that have occurred before negative forces arise. This includes preventing further violations of Diné Fundamental Law that exist to keep hózhǫ́ among the people and the land called home. Knowing that we cannot go back in time, we move forward hoping that we learn from our past mistakes. The Diyin Dine'é knew that people would make mistakes and made ceremonies available to make necessary corrections. Diné Fundamental Law was also given to the Diné so that they can maintain balance in their journey of life.

If we don't correct our actions and bring healing back to our homelands, we will further endanger our people, animals, and the environment. Nahasdzáán Nihimá will make necessary changes to heal and stop the pain she endures. This can be in the form of natural disasters, changes in the ecosystem, imbalance in the weather and the seasons, loss of herbal medicine and food sources, and loss of our Diné due to sickness. Lessons from our previous worlds serve as examples.

Damage to our homelands will also impact the Diné in socio-economic issues that include failure of economic development and job loss, higher crime rates, health issues, and long-term poverty. This would result in an exodus of young Diné from their communities and families that would lead to the loss of Diné culture and language. That would prevent us from showing our true identity as granted by the Holy People, and we would lose our ceremonies. These are harsh realities that the Diné people could face in the future.

But I have hope for our future, regardless of our current situation, because I see more of our people understanding the value of our Diné culture and the importance of incorporating Diné Fundamental Law into our everyday lives. These are steps in the right direction for ourselves, our future generations, and the world around us. There are many larger issues coming up, and this issue with our land can be something we can resolve if it is a priority for ourselves.

I am hoping that as more Diné people understand how interconnected all our cultural values are, they will preserve our oral traditional stories and our ceremonies. I also would emphasize the importance of keeping these sacred teachings in line with the Diné Fundamental Law that guides the Diné to observe certain ceremonies in the summer season and others in the winter season.

For Diné all this begins with each individual, as part of our traditional law states that we govern ourselves and we have the intelligence to make decisions to value ourselves as children of the Diyin Dine'é. The direction we choose to take reflects on our understanding of how we acknowledge ourselves to our Mother Earth and Father Sky, and the Holy People who are our sovereign deities.

CHAPTER 2

Dinétahdi Kéédahwiit'įnígíí
Ayóo Danihidziil

MARIO ATENCIO

Nitsáhákees

Yá'át'ééh, Hashtł'ishnii nishłį́; Tódích'íí'nii báshíshchíín; Ta'neeszahnii dashicheii; Tł'ááshchí'í dashinálí. Na'neelzhiin hoolyéedę́ę́' kééhasht'į́. I am of the Mud Clan, born to the Bitter Water Clan. My maternal grandfather's mothers are of the Tangle People; my paternal grandfather's mothers are of the "upper-area-of-the-face, painted-red" clan.

As I write this chapter, I am the vice-president of Na'neelzhiin (Torreon/Starlake) Chapter. If the Navajo Nation is considered a hooghan, bounded and supported by the six sacred mountains, then far eastern chapters of Na'neelzhiin, Counselors, and Ojo Encino should be considered the keepers of the doorway.

Na'neelzhiin is the farthest eastern Diné community on the Navajo Nation. Na'neelzhiin is part of the ancient Diné holy lands of Dinétah.[1] These lands are home to ancient stories of our emergence into this world. Across all these stories, Nahasdzáán (Mother Earth) and Yádiłhił (Father Sky) are living entities, and we, as humans, are wholly dependent on the greater being to provide elements for life the world provides.[2]

Local leaders from the Dinétah region are some of the earliest named Diné in written history.[3] Leaders in the Na'neelzhiin/Dinétah region have led a centuries-long resistance to European imperial and colonial efforts to gain control of lands.[4] The most important of these articles is the "Big Bead Mesa: Where Campfires Burned in the Ancient Days" article, as it is a very rare documentation of the Na'neelzhiin region-specific oral history, as told by a local medicine man.[5]

This oral history showcases the long-standing theme of resistance and the need of the Na'neelzhiin peoples to stand with integrity in the face of immense pressure caused by war against the Spanish Empire and the Pueblo Nations. These histories fit into the theme of Diné resistance to settler-colonial moves to gain control of the land.[6]

Na'neelzhiin Diné have long engaged in efforts to gain back control of the land. In the current time, it seems that we are experiencing highly effectual dynamic shifting environmental, political, economic, and cultural phenomena (global climate change, global pandemic, megadrought, oil and gas development, social upheaval and change, etc.). If we slowed down and explained what is happening in the Diné way of thinking, holding onto the land and protecting it becomes extremely important.[7]

This chapter applies a Diné methodology to understand the nuances of how the people from the Na'neelzhiin region perceive the land. Through the example of an ecological disaster caused by the oil and gas industry, I examine how Dinétah people have created a resistance movement that centers the protection and control of the lands, which we view as central to the continuation of Diné community in Dinétah. The chapter is structured into four sections, following the educational philosophy of Sá'ah Naagháíí Bik'eh Hózhóǫn (SNBH) and the Nitsáhákees, Nahat'á, Iiná, and Siihasin processes.[8] Navajo and Diné will be used interchangeably.

Nahatá

This chapter will analyze an event where significant amounts of toxic crude oil and toxic waste were spilled on lands in the Dinétah region to explain the unique "checkerboarded" jurisdiction of the Dinétah region and the efforts to solve this complex issue. Amid this land problem is the story of how the local Dinétah people generated a highly visible grassroots-led coalition that gained the support of the highest levels of the U.S. government. This coalition also engaged and was successful in federal litigation. In total, this chapter will show that the Dinétah people have a deep cultural legacy of leading the resistance to injustice and demanding their human rights, and this legacy is an empowering framework for land, air, water, and spiritual protection for future generations of Diné.

FIGURE 2.1 Oil and produced water spill site in relation to the Chaco Culture National Historical Park

Some sources for this chapter are written by non-Diné white men and women who "translated" and/or analyzed all the primary source materials.[9] This chapter privileges oral histories as primary sources, and those stories are held by the people. Any misrepresentations and inconsistencies that may arise will be my responsibility to rectify according to community-based protocols.

Iiná

In February 2019, nearly 59,000 gallons of crude oil and toxic waste (produced water) spilled onto the lands held by my father's family in the Counselor Chapter of the Dinétah region.[10] The spill flowed about a mile downstream into the Escavada Wash, which flows into the Chaco Culture National Historical Park (CCNHP).

Figure 2.2 is a snapshot of the complex land holdings in the Dinétah region. Here are represented four land statuses, but in the region, there are more than eleven different land statuses.[11] There is New Mexico State Trust land, individual Indian allotted land, public domain managed by the Bureau of Land Management, and Navajo tribal trust land surface with the underlying mineral still owned by the United States public and managed by the Bureau of Land Management. The official body that deals with this is the Eastern Navajo Land Commission. The regulatory history of the checkerboarded Dinétah is succinctly documented in Soni Grant's first chapter in "Patchwork: Land, Law, and Extraction in the Greater Chaco."[12]

This incident happened in an area known to the people called Ásaa' Si'ą́ą́n, "Where the pot is sitting." According to local stories, there was a spring that flowed into a large pottery vessel. The area was a pilgrimage stopping point for Diné people to fill their water bags as they made pilgrimages to the holy mountains in the region and into Colorado. According to the final report regarding the spill, which my family has never formally received (nor have we had any communication with the state regulatory agencies), the groundwater is now contaminated, and all these actions are not necessarily against any laws or regulations.[13]

The Navajo Nation has received Treatment as State (TAS) status when it comes to the Safe Drinking Water and Clean Air Act, meaning that the U.S. Environmental Protection Agency (EPA) regulations and jurisdiction extends to within the boundaries of the Eastern Navajo Agency, re-

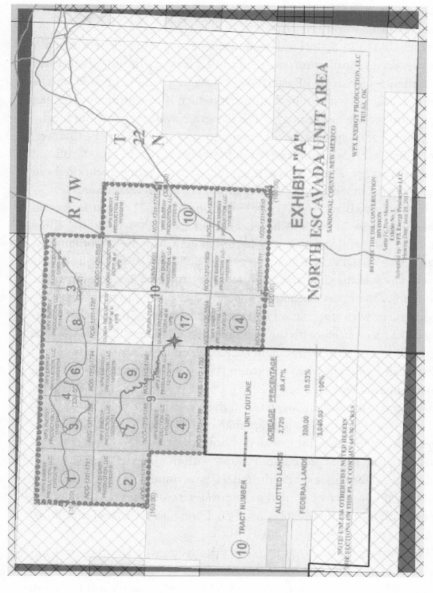

FIGURE 2.2 Counselor chapter map from April 2019 oil and produced water incident report sent to New Mexico Environment Department

gardless of land status.[14] The spill has violated the Navajo Nation's Safe
Drinking Water Act, yet the Navajo Nation EPA has not responded to
repeated attempts by email to review the incident and weigh in on the
impacts caused by oil and gas.

From 2013 to 2015, the local communities engaged in a legislative initiative to push for the moratorium of oil and gas leasing. The initial successes
were the passage of two Eastern Navajo Agency Council resolutions, a
regional council, with limited authority, which is to coordinate regional
legislation for the betterment of the Eastern Navajo Agency. But locally
the Counselor Chapter, a sister community of Torreon/Starlake Chapter,
concluded that those efforts were not having enough effect on the oil and
gas development. The oil and gas operators were operating unchecked and
causing environmental and cultural impacts to the local communities.[15]

So, when the Black Mesa Water Coalition on October 24, 2015, hosted
a meeting at the Counselor Chapter and had Kandi Mosset-White, Three
Affiliated Tribes oil and gas activist, present to the Counselor community,
a collective of eight matriarchs demanded action to stop the oil and gas
development in the Counselor Community.[16] The next day, a group of five
community members formed a collective that started to meet regularly
to discuss how to stop the oil and gas development. The local community had a relationship with the venerable Navajo nonprofit Diné Citizens
Against Ruining our Environment (C.A.R.E.) and the community gained
substantial legal help when the group started working with the Western
Environmental Law Center (WELC). Over time, the group, through in-
tensive grassroots organizing, built on the work started, and the Counsel-
or's based movement grew to more than two hundred local, national, and
international organizations, which is now known as the Greater Chaco
Coalition. The local community groups, with the help of Diné C.A.R.E.
and WELC, won a case where the federal government did not adequately
consider the impact of oil and gas on water resources and greenhouse
gases.[17] This meant the Greater Chaco Coalition now spearheads the global
climate justice movement.

Legislatively, with key outreach and negotiation with New Mexico Congressional leadership, who occupy a key leadership position in the U.S.
House of Representatives and Senate, a congressional bill was passed in
2019 to protect a ten-mile buffer around the CCNHP. This bill would fail in
the U.S. Senate because the Natural Resource Committee was controlled

by the Republicans. Administratively, the Greater Chaco Coalition's advocacy helped convince Secretary of the Interior David Bernhardt to defer oil and gas leasing within the Greater Chaco Landscape.[18] This was significant because this was during the Trump administration, and for Secretary Bernhardt to defer leases in the Greater Chaco Landscape was counter to the administration's neoliberal "Energy Dominance" agenda.

In response to successful Greater Chaco Coalition organizing, the oil and gas companies got the Navajo Nation Council to become adversarial to our coalition.[19] The Biden administration ran on a campaign promise to "[ban] new oil and gas permitting on public lands and water," and the administration has been placed in check by the oil and gas industry lawsuits. Now the administration must make political decisions to limit any more real engagement on this issue.[20] These developments have limited a lot of the momentum we have built since 2015. From our perspective, after years of hard work and hope, we begrudgingly realize this was always the end-game reality.

This spill, and the reality of how ineffective the U.S. federal actions are, has now caused a need for a paradigm shift because we must see oil and gas pollution and desecration of the land, air, water, and sacred places as a direct threat to future generations' ability to survive in the coming climate crisis. This shift is to critically understand how we have not been effective and how we must truly engage to protect the land, air, water, and sacred places. Is this new paradigm continuing down the legislative/litigious paths?

This paradigm shift will have to ask existence, via ceremony, for guidance on what steps are needed.[21] There must be an understanding of how deeply impactful global climate change is going to be and what social changes the people will have to endure. This paradigm needs to be cynical about the United States honoring its past treaties and agreements when it comes to water resources.[22] This is different from the Greater Chaco Coalition organizing actions, which rely on U.S. domestic litigious relief. The future climate change–caused social upheaval might be the beginning of arbitrary motions by the United States to protect its power. Water resources are essential to this power.

What this paradigm shift must consider are the implications of a climate "changeover." Diné medicine man John Holiday tells of an ancient prophecy that defines this changeover as when the seasons will shorten and then change places.[23] There are a few published sources that openly discuss this changeover, and the sources found cite anecdotal evidence that the seasons are starting to shift.[24] If the above prophecy is starting to come true, then the people will have to be reminded that life is not supposed to be as easy as the last sixty years have been. The young people will become strong-willed and hearty people. In this way, they will be more like our ancestors than we ever will be. The paradigm needs to not just be lawsuits but political, physical actions that protect all the elements of life. The young people will need to look to the mountains for leadership. The next generations will be like the mountains.

Our actions to protect the land, air, water, and sacred places can show the deep love we have for Nahasdzáán. Our Diné values are embedded in all our actions. The future leaders in the next half of this century and beyond will have to deal with our failures. The land will drive these new methods for the paradigm shift. Through a deep understanding of our past prayers, we will gain understanding of the best way forward.[25] In the middle of a megadrought, who are the powerful? The people with water will drive policy, and our actions today are nowhere near what is needed to protect the water. I believe the people in the future will look at the sacred places and take decisive action by not just using the Navajo Nation's Safe Drinking Water Act, but the other beings/elements that reveal themselves as wanting to join the fight. But the people with the humble power to grow/gather food and live with a minimal amount of water will be the inheritors of the land in the future.

Siihasin

The Dinétah people have been resisting empires, republics, and democracies' actions to gain more land and power. We have been at the frontline of these fights since the seventeenth century. In the future, the young people will be looking for permission to speak out, and they will see that the Dinétah/Na'neelzhiin people have always been a community with deeply ingrained values that seeks and expects the right to determine its own future. Even with the checkerboard land status challenges, the Dinétah people have started an impactful environmental justice process to lead the Indigenous fight against the climate change crisis. The process has been so successful that the president of the United States even can be counted as a champion of their cause.[26] This would seem to be a great achievement, but the reality is that it is not enough, and a new method must arise. The land, air, water, and the sacred places, themselves, will tell how this will be done.

Notes

1. John Redhouse, *Holy Land: A Navajo Pilgrimage Back to Dinétah* (Albuquerque, N.M.: Redhouse/Wright Productions, 1985), 4.

2. "The Fundamental Laws of the Diné," accessed November 20, 2013, http://www .navajocourts.org/dine.htm.

3. Richard Van Valkenburgh, "Navajo Naat'aáni," *Kiva* 13, no. 2 (January 1, 1948): 6.

4. Frank McNitt, *Navajo Wars: Military Campaigns, Slave Raids, and Reprisals* (Albuquerque: University of New Mexico Press, 1990), 6; Peter Iverson and Monty Roessel, *Diné: A History of the Navajos* (Albuquerque: University of New Mexico Press, 2002), 25.

5. Richard Van Valkenburgh, "Big Bead Mesa: Where Campfires Burned in the Ancient Days," *The Desert Magazine*, February 1945, 6.

6. Patrick Wolfe, "Settler Colonialism and the Elimination of the Native," *Journal of Genocide Research* 8, no. 4 (2006): 387.

7. "The Fundamental Laws of the Diné."

8. Mario Atencio, "A Diné Conceptualization of Global Climate Change: An Application of a Diné Research Methodology" (master of science, Arizona State University, 2015), 14, http://search.proquest.com.ezproxy1.lib.asu.edu/docview/167 9455692?pq-origsite=summon.

9. Susan B. Brill de Ramirez, "The Resistance of American Indian Autobiographies to Ethnographic Colonization," *Mosaic: A Journal for the Interdisciplinary Study of Literature (Univ. of Manitoba, Winnipeg)* 32, no. 2 (1999): 59.

10. Jerry Redfern, "Fracking Brings Pollution, Not Wealth to Navajo Land," March 30, 2021, https://capitalandmain.com/fracking-brings-pollution-not-wealth-to-navajo -land-0329.

11. "EplanningUi," accessed May 22, 2022, https://eplanning.blm.gov/eplanning-ui /project/2016892/580.

12. Sonia Alexandrine Porelle Grant, "Patchwork: Land, Law, and Extraction in the Greater Chaco" (PhD diss., University of Chicago, n.d.), 53, https://doi.org/10 .6082/uchicago.2832.

13. Redfern, "Fracking Brings Pollution, Not Wealth to Navajo Land."

14. Navajo Nation Environmental Protection Agency, "Navajo Nation Environmental Protection Agency (NNEPA)," Navajo Nation Environmental Protection Agency, accessed May 23, 2022, https://navajoepa.org/.

15. David J. Tsosie et al., "A Cultural, Spiritual and Health Impact Assessment of Oil Drilling Operations in the Navajo Nation Area of Counselor, Torreon and Ojo Encino Chapters," 2021.

16. "Dooda Fracking—Posts | Facebook," accessed May 22, 2022, https://www.face book.com/doodafracking.nn/posts/1123470337678042; "Greater Chaco Coalition Celebrates New Path Forward for Landscape Protection," *Western Environmental Law Center* (blog), November 15, 2021, https://westernlaw.org/greater-chaco-coalition-celebrates-new-path-forward-landscape-protection/.

17. "Protecting Chaco Canyon and the San Juan Basin from Fracking," *Western Environmental Law Center* (blog), accessed May 23, 2022, https://westernlaw.org/protecting-chaco-canyon-san-juan-basin-fracking/.

18. "Oil, Gas Leases Near Chaco Canyon Deferred after David Bernhardt Visit," accessed May 23, 2022, https://www.daily-times.com/story/news/local/2019/05/29/oil-gas-leases-near-chaco-canyon-deferred-after-david-bernhardt-visit/1272552001/.

19. Danielle Prokop (dprokop@sfnewmexican.com), "Navajo Nation Council Demands Smaller Buffer Around Chaco," Santa Fe New Mexican, accessed May 23, 2022, https://www.santafenewmexican.com/news/local_news/navajo-nation-council-demands-smaller-buffer-around-chaco/article_3362782e-3ee4-11ea-9e48-0b90b8f17a01.html.

20. "Biden Vowed to Ban New Drilling on Public Lands. It Won't Be Easy," *Washington Post*, accessed May 23, 2022, https://www.washingtonpost.com/climate-environment/2020/11/19/biden-climate-change-drilling/.

21. Atencio, "A Diné Conceptualization of Global Climate Change," 42.

22. "The Colorado River Is Drying Up. Here's How That Affects Indigenous Water Rights," Grist, October 6, 2021, https://grist.org/equity/colorado-river-drought-indigenous-water-rights/.

23. John Holiday and Robert S. McPherson, *A Navajo Legacy: The Life and Teachings of John Holiday* (Norman: University of Oklahoma Press, 2011), 285.

24. Atencio, "A Diné Conceptualization of Global Climate Change," 24.

25. Atencio, "A Diné Conceptualization of Global Climate Change," 42–43.

26. Mario Atencio et al., "Federal Statutes and Environmental Justice in the Navajo Nation: The Case of Fracking in the Greater Chaco Region," *American Journal of Public Health* 112, no. 1 (January 2022): 116–23, https://doi.org/10.2105/AJPH.2021.306562.

SHÁDI'ÁÁH / SOUTH

Summer on Nihikéyah. Courtesy of Lloyd L. Lee.

CHAPTER 3

Form, Memory

Mapping Land Through Diné Poetry

JAKE SKEETS

When asked to discuss Dinétah through my perspective, I think of two things: form and memory. Forms, vessels, and containers can be understood as a kind of scaffolding one follows during composition and design. Memory, through the scope of this chapter, exists in a higher dimensional space related to space and time. This chapter will examine the approaches to land as form and land as memory within Diné poetry as a way to define Dinétics, or Diné aesthetics and poetics. The critical interventions made by Diné poets shine a light on our relationship with the land and further define the idea of *homeland*. Diné thought and lifeways are already composites with land at their center. We see their presence in the very aesthetics and poetics of Diné life: Blue Bird Flour bags, Diné cornstalk models, architectural design on Navajo, and elsewhere. This essay, then, will look at the way Diné poetries have intervened in our relationship with land in the hopes that it will trigger further interventions into the way land is mapped within a variety of disciplines and professions. After all, land exists everywhere, and it has an innate capacity to inform the various processes of Diné and non-Diné communities globally. Reframing land as fundamental to our perception of reality will help classify it as part of our personhood and our interior and domestic spaces. Often we can look to poets to make these critical interventions possible as the poem becomes a site for the interrogation of language itself, and it is through language that we build and code our realities. It is through language that we can further sculpt the idea of a *home*land. The emphasis of home is necessary, as it is often considered to be where thought begins. These interventions allow all land to be considered homeland and therefore protected from further extraction and destruction.

Land as Form

Diné poet Esther Belin and her poetics have often interrogated land and form. In her poem "Before We Ever Begin," Belin uses land as form by using text and punctuation to illustrate the Chuska Mountains.[1] Often known as concrete poetry, I argue that land as form is a constraint that is beyond Western poetic forms and is employed by Diné poets because of the way land informs form and not the way Western constructions inform language. Denise Levertov, in her essay "Some Notes on Organic Form," writes that organic form "is the concept that there is a form in all things (and in our experience) which the poet can discover and reveal."[2] Levertov argues that organic poetry is a "method of apperception," borrowing from Gerard Manley Hopkins's work on inscape, wherein poetry is exploratory by nature and is a result of the gathering of our perceptions into a singular form. To write poetry like this, Levertov states that "there must be an experience, a sequence or constellation of perceptions of sufficient interest, felt by the poet intensely enough to demand of him their equivalence in words: he is brought to speech."[3] Levertov is examining the openness of organic form as opposed to constricted conventional forms in Western-based poetry.

In Western-based poetics, the romance of formal poetry is taught as foundational to learning how to write poetry. However, Levertov is arguing that there is an initiating force and an organic and forceful response within the poet to write words down in a manner of "intuitive interaction between all the elements involved."[4] Levertov continues, "In the same way, content and form are in a state of dynamic interaction; the understanding of whether an experience is a linear sequence or a constellation raying out from and into a central focus or axis, for instance, is discoverable only in the work, not before it."[5] Language is the product of land, and Levertov continues that argument here to posit that poetry, then, is also a product of land. Diné poetries often operate similarly, as a collection of poems born out of the land itself.

In the opening piece to *Flood Song*, the second book by Diné poet Sherwin Bitsui, the word Tó is repeated and centered down the field of the page.[6] In the book, one can see the way language is responding to the land and the organic nature of the universe around us. The forces that exist within land spark various interventions by Diné poets that result in a reconstruction of what I call "page politics," a series of colonial standards that dictate and codify proper literacy for Native people. Page politics exist to ensure that Diné ways of thinking are marginalized, and colonial codes dominate the way Diné people read and write. Belin and Bitsui both challenge page politics by stepping into the field of the page and intervening in the way the text is read. There is a push outward and beyond the left margin—the colonial understanding of where text starts. This push away from the left margin appears to be a constant thread within Dinétics. In her poem "Tsoodził, Mountain in the South," Laura Tohe, the second Navajo Nation poet laureate, arranges the ending words of the poem in a diagonal line. It reads:

> your sweet music
> pouring forth like
>   rain
>
>   rain
>
>   rain
>
>   rain . . .[7]

There is a disruption of the left margin and favor of the centered and right margin. Within page politics, the critical intervention being made here is to bring the subject (speaker and poet) and object (content, language, and reader) out from what is considered proper and toward what is considered organic. These poets and their critical interventions using a kind of concrete poetry distill the idea of land as form. However, the push against page politics offers a new strategy Diné poets use to resist colonialism and forge land as form, which is foundational in a Diné-centric view of the world.

It should be noted that the formation of a Dinétics does not infer that all Diné poets write the same poetry. Belin, Bitsui, and Tohe all write poetry in vastly different ways but remain committed to a similar kind of resistance. While these poets push against the left margin, other poets are examining the literal flow of language and using page politics to craft important interventions. Diné poet Norla Chee, in her poem "Spirit

Mountains," uses the margin to resist the way we understand prose within her work. While prose as a colonial construction mimics the idea of the paragraph, we see here a reimagining of the paragraph as a vessel of momentary thoughts or sensations. There is not a will for rhetoric within these vessels but rather a window toward the organic. Chee writes:

> On Rain Mountain, made of turquoise,
> the flute and howling wind surround me in beauty.
>   with
>   cedar
>   I   it[8]
>   bless

Land as form here is resisting the colonial containers of margin and paragraph and allows Chee to move freely into the organic space. The language moves through punctuation and space with ease as if song or prayer. There is a circuitry present within the poem that electrifies its presentation and reading.

In an interview titled "The Circuitry of Poetics," Sherwin Bitsui states, "A poem guides you. It guides you into spaces or scenes and images that are sometimes difficult to see. The strategies for creating a poem or the ways that I use the verbs, is that the whole world has some force and energy to it. Even language can move you towards something."[9] Again, the notion of an organic force moving through composition is repeated here by Bitsui. Bitsui's argument for a kind of natural composition in regard to a verb is one carried forward by a reverence for the landscape. Diné weavers have often used the idea of land as form in their construction, composition, and design of rugs. It's not illuminated as Diné concrete poems, but there is a hidden energy that exists within rugs that can be seen and felt. In fact, touching a rug can tell a story about the weaving process: where a mistake might have happened, where the warp was too tight, where it began, and where the weft touches. Poems can offer something similar.

The movement away from the margin is as much as a response to hidden forces as it is a resistance to coloniality. In her poem "Sometimes Those Pueblo Men Can Sure Be Coyotes," Tohe creates a back-and-forth relationship with the left margin. Some lines kiss the margin and others push away. It reads:

This time Mister Kayate drove up
  in the gray "G-car," the government car
    that's what we called it
    and we had to call the men mister[10]

The subsequent lines are moved a space away from the left margin before the poem returns to it. This movement back and forth is creating an energy within the piece. I call this form Yilk'oł form, named after the kinetics of wave formations. The orbital motion of a wave is like the orbital motion of the sun traveling across the sky. In fact, gravity is the reason for both phenomena. The circular motion continues because of the very physics of the universe. The poem's form is sparked into existence as a kind of synonymous relationship with physics and an emergence out of the land. Language, then, verbs the poem into motion. The form has been used since the early start of contemporary Diné poetry. Nia Francisco is a poet who can be considered one of the early poets to get work published and has subsequently shaped entire generations of Diné poets. In her poem "ode to a drunk woman," Francisco's lines move between the left margin and center space, which provides a look like the step design of Diné baskets.[11] There are also the sounds, images, and verbs that drive the reader forward along the wavelengths of the poem. Once moved away from the left margin, the poem continues outward for a time before its descent back to the left margin. This friction creates a momentum within the poem. The poem ends away from the left margin that constructs the poetic line here as a force raying out from its initial spark.

Land as Memory

I've written before that land is wrapped in a memory field, a spatial-temporal matrix of land, time, memory, and language.[12] The memory field is an argument that land is a holder of memory and, therefore, becomes part of the domestic space. In this essay, I hope to extend this argument to posit that land is memory, and Diné poets have always approached land as memory. This reclamation of land then reclassifies land as a matter of the interior. To provide a wide survey of Diné poetry, we can also examine a couple of emerging Diné poets to see the way Dinétics continues to be shaped by new voices. Diné poet Paige Buffington published a prose poem, titled "Sites," in which we see the way memory and land are always woven together. The poem reads, "Hills rise and roll, brown and lonely like the saddle the family's oldest uncle left."[13] The metaphor between the hills and the uncle's saddle is designed and composed by Buffington with purpose. The hills become the saddle; the land becomes the memory. The poem continues, "This is the wash where relatives took the mattresses of the dead and dying to burn—where cousins gathered to shoot bottles, old dishes, the dogs that kill four sheep."[14] Again, the wash is transformed into the memory of these stories: family who have passed, cousins gathering to shoot bottles, and dogs that killed the sheep. The speaker's perception of their reality is shaped by the landscape. The land becomes the lens through which they see the world. This conceptualization of the land as a matter of the thought process illustrates the way land is uniquely woven with our most intimate and interior spaces. This is important to understand in the reframing of all land as homeland.

Tacey Atsitty's debut collection *Rain Scald* is a meditation on land, the body, and memory. The poems take us away from the Navajo Nation as the poems interact with other landscapes outside the reservation. However, Atsitty is still able to create a kind of homeland in these off-reservation spaces because of the way the land is connected to home and our interior selves. In her poem "Sunbeam," the speaker is remembering a family accident, but the land within it is formed into elements of the memory. The poem reads, "Our two vehicles leave the Chuskas. I want a sucker. Cheii takes me south. There are six of them in the other car; they turn north. It is too bright today. Two weeks ago, my mom dreamt of night birds chanting amid juniper berries. Today, the land formations look like owls."[15] The metaphor here conflates the land and the memory, but this time we get only elements of the memory. This creates a kind of physical distance between the event itself and the circumstances of the speaker. However, the poem is able to maintain a sense of belonging through the small gestures of memory, land, and story. For example, the car involved in the accident is the car that turns north, a direction one does not face when sleeping according to Diné thought. Then, the land forming into owls illustrates another reach for a lineage both present and nonpresent. The land becomes the connection to a Diné worldview. If we take another leap in time and examine one of the most acclaimed Diné poets today, we can see the way all land, even land outside the reservation, can be constructed as a homeland. Luci Tapahonso has created a very important career in poetry and remains one of the forefront voices in Diné poetry, even serving as the inaugural Navajo Nation poet laureate. Her poem "It Is a Simple Story" supports the notion that land becomes a place of connection to Diné worldview that weaves timelines together, often calming the grief alive in past experiences. The poem reads:

These hills surround us in all shades of brown of gray.
It is in this calmness, in the pale sky above,
and in the wind grazing at our clothes and hair
that I feel the quiet loneliness of the dead in this vast place,
and I know that we are with them,

together and apart.[16]

Land as memory tells us that the homeland is possible everywhere, as the speaker of the poem is in Kansas and not on the Navajo Nation. Memory enables land to become apparent in all spaces and even in all things. Land becomes the material around us through memory. These ideas are not new, of course. I think they are somewhat organic in the Diné worldview. I believe this because of the work of Diné poet, healer, scholar, and former Navajo Nation Vice President Rex Lee Jim.

Rex Lee Jim, in his poem "A Grandmother's Memory," illustrates the land's capacity for processing trauma and grief by transforming it into a tool. He writes:

Tears run down grooves of aged skin
Glistening in the dying light
Dusk slides away with fading
Memories that only
Sounds of the weaving stick
Could hold on to[17]

Here land is transformed into a tool for remembering the speaker, and the speaker's grandmother shares a moment of reflection of a grandfather. The grandfather's existence is made possible for the speaker and the speaker's grandmother through the weaving stick and loom, which are both materials of the land itself. Now the land has seeped into the materials of our lives. Through land as memory, land also becomes everything around us. Because land is so connected to both interior and exterior processes, land is both *home*land and *thought*land. In his poem "The Caravan," Sherwin Bitsui details the way land and objects considered opposite to land are actually both part of the organic when engaged with memory and thought. The poem reads:

> The city's neon embers
> stripe the asphault's blank page
> where this story pens itself nightly,
> where ghosts weave their oily hair
> into his belt of ice,
> dress him in pleated shadows[18]

The city, paranormal, and even clothes are transformed into materials of the land: embers, hair, ice, and shadows. The memory here is functioning both as subject but also as the poem's guiding force that births the images and sounds within the poem. When approaching land as memory, the ability to redefine land's relationship to the self deepens. Land becomes storyteller by holding onto memories. Land becomes altar by holding onto the grief and emotional turmoil of our pasts. Land also becomes all the materials of our daily existence, with which a reality is forged, a *thought*land. Land becomes part of our being and a matter of the domestic, a *home*land. This is opposite to land's colonial designation as wilderness, which left it open to destructive and extractive forces. Therefore, land as memory is a call to protect the land itself.

Opportunities

What interventions exist within poetry that have us reunderstand our organic reality? If poetries of an organic form, read as outside a Western-based romanticized form, are indeed land as form and land as memory, how does a poem, as a site for intervention and interrogation of language, jolt what it means to witness the world? Diné poet Orlando White, in his poem "Nascent," writes:

Pronunciation marks are proof
        of one's own cultural sentience.

Those authentic reverberations
        above the cap height where breath

pressures tongue against teeth
        below the baseline where throat

exhales the long access vowel
        in that moment it echoes through

nose, quivers as phonemic air:
        the ogonek tickle of   łį́į́'[19]

Here we see Diné Bizaad as informed by organics that exist within the world. The word *łį́į́'* is a result of comparisons between the human and animal body, the human and natural world, connected by sound, as illuminated by White. The human self is connected to the universe and its organics through sound. Or perhaps we can read it as the first line argues: that pronunciation and sound prove sentience. In a review of the collection *Dark Thirty* by Santee Frazier, White suggests, "This idea of transforming sound into being is interesting when we consider that the word 'person' is formed from *per-* which means *through* or *by means of* and *son* which is the root of 'sound.'"[20] When broken down by sound, "person" could mean "through sound" or "by means of sound." So, to be a human person means to exist by way of sound. Where is sound born? Sound is born from the land because language is a product of the land. The sounds we make and hear stem from the sounds that exist within the land itself. Land as form and memory ultimately shows us our innate connection to it. This seems like a simple gesture, but the smallest shifts in consciousness can help catalyze larger shifts elsewhere. It helped me realize that my homeland for me exists everywhere. No matter where I am traveling, I am always in the process of going home.

    I wrote before about the impact Diné lands have for me as a person, thinker, and poet. Driving home from Albuquerque through Grants and Gallup has always been the best way to let go of stress and tension built up inside my body. The sight of the pink and red cliffsides against the setting sun remind me, each time, that I am home, that there exists part of my being in the lands. Settler colonialism, through language, altered relations with the land by naming land as external, empty, uncivilized, and savage. To reap the benefits of extraction and erasure, those in power needed a story that the land somehow was opposite to domesticity, not worthy of protection. However, Indigenous people have been protecting homelands for generations, combating the very notion that the land is somehow void of breath. This chapter is an attempt to reclassify our relationship with land as part of our domestic space, as *home*land. A homeland is both a home place, as defined by Larry Evers and Ofelia Zepeda,[21] and land connected to the domesticity of the natural and cosmic world—all relations intertwined, remembered, and empowered. It also defines land as *thought*-land wherein language is a result of land and not the other way around. It's through a landscape language that human people are given the capacity to understand their own existence. I come to think of it as an early morning in Tsaile, a rambler night in Gallup, or a calm drive to Junction in Chinle. The land has a way of speaking to us and somewhere we began to listen.

Notes

1. Esther Belin, *Of Cartography* (Tucson: University of Arizona Press, 2017), 18.
2. Denise Levertov, "Some Notes on Organic Form," Poetry Foundation, reprinted October 13, 2009, https://www.poetryfoundation.org/articles/69392/some-notes-on-organic-form-56d249032078f, par. 1.
3. Denise Levertov, "Some Notes on Organic Form," par. 3.
4. Denise Levertov, "Some Notes on Organic Form," par. 5.
5. Denise Levertov, "Some Notes on Organic Form," par. 6.
6. Sherwin Bitsui, *Flood Song* (Port Townsend: Copper Canyon Press, 2009).
7. Laura Tohe, "Tsoodził, Mountain in the South," in *The Diné Reader*, ed. Esther Belin, Jeff Berglund, Connie A. Jacobs, and Anthony K. Webster (Tucson: University of Arizona Press, 2021), 131.
8. Norla Chee, *Cedar Smoke on Abalone Mountain* (Los Angeles: UCLA American Indian Studies Center, 2001), 46.
9. Sarah Aronson, "The Circuitry of Poetics with Sherwin Bitsui," Montana Public Radio, October 25, 2018, https://www.mtpr.org/arts-culture/2018-10-25/the-circuitry-of-poetics-with-sherwin-bitsui.
10. Laura Tohe, *No Parole Today* (Albuquerque: West End Press, 1999), 16.
11. Nia Francisco, "ode to a drunk woman," in *The Diné Reader*, eds. Esther Belin, Jeff Berglund, Connie A. Jacobs, and Anthony K. Webster (Tucson: University of Arizona Press, 2021), 61–62.

12. Jake Skeets, "The Memory Field," *Emergence Magazine*, October 14, 2020, https:// emergencemagazine.org/essay/the-memory-field.

13. Paige Buffington, "Sites," *Terrain.org*, June 28, 2019, https://www.terrain.org /2019/poetry/paige-buffington, par. 1.

14. Buffington, "Sites," par. 2.

15. Tacey Atsitty, *Rain Scald* (Albuquerque: University of New Mexico Press, 2018), 8.

16. Luci Tapahonso, *Sáanii Dahataał: The Women Are Singing* (Tucson: University of Arizona Press, 1993), 38.

17. Rex Lee Jim, *Saad Lá Tah Hózhóón: A Collection of Diné Poetry* (Flagstaff: Salina Bookshelf, 2019), 41.

18. Sherwin Bitsui, *Dissolve* (Port Townsend: Copper Canyon Press, 2019), 4.

19. Orlando White, *LETTERRS* (Brooklyn: Nightboat Books, 2015), 17.

20. Orlando White, "To Find the Subject by Leaving the Subject: Expectations of Race & Content," *Harriet Blog*, November 12, 2015, Poetry Foundation, https:// www.poetryfoundation.org/harriet-books/2015/11/to-find-the-subject-by-leaving -the-subject-expectations-of-race-content, par. 4.

21. Larry Evers and Ofelia Zepeda, *Home Places: Contemporary Native American Writing from Sun Tracks* (Tucson: University of Arizona Press, 1995).

CHAPTER 4

"My Breath Is Rain Essence"

Ruminations on Rain, Land, Language, Time, and Storytelling in Diné Thought

MANNY LOLEY

for my family

From My Home

Contemplating my connection to land conjures within me the mesas surrounding my home, summers hauling wood, and monsoon rains with streaming floods in the place that nurtured my growth. From my home in Tsétah Tó Ak'ólí, a bundle of mesas rises in the east, over high desert fields unfurling with díwózhii, tsá'ászi ts'óóz, and tsédédééh. Gáagii Bighan towers over the shorter mesa shimásání called Tsé Chį́į́h Łichíí' Da'azkáni. Nídíshchíí' and gad are scattered all over both mesas, their twisting trunks and evergreen branches a constant through all seasons. Below these mesas is my old Grandma Mary's cornfield. Shimá often recounts stories about harvesting corn pollen with my old Grandma Mary in the summer; how my old Grandma Mary would carry a big silver bowl with her, shaking the golden tassels into the depths of the bowl until bright flecks of corn pollen dusted the bottom. All the while, my old Grandma Mary would sing and talk to the plants, asking for good health and to bless the family many generations from where she stood. Although I never met my old Grandma Mary, I think about shimá's stories and memories of her often, about how her prayers and words and thoughts carried our family forward, and I imagine her voice settling into the land I call home.

In the south, the mountain at Bluewater Lake appears as a dark blue nub with flashing towers. Me, shínaaí, and shiye' Jaiden prepare for the winter months early, trekking up the mountain in June and July to gather firewood. We leave our home in the early morning, with breakfast bur-

ritos, coffee, and water in hand, and by noon or early afternoon, we've
filled both shínaaí's truck and shitsilí's truck with firewood. Shitsilí is a
Marine, and he is stationed in Japan. Sometimes he will video call and add
his voice to the sound of wood being chopped, laughter, and the stories
shínaaí tells of our cheii, who valued hard work and ingenuity. Our cheii
was the most innovative and capable person in our lives, and from him, my
brothers learned to solve any issue. In seasons when piñons cluster in their
reddish-brown splendor, shimá and shimásání will accompany us up the
mountain with their coffee cans and empty Blue Bird Flour sacks. While
they pick piñons beneath squat trees, shimá often tells more stories about
my old Grandma Mary and how she used to crawl under the lowest tree
branches where no one wanted to pick, her skirt visible from beneath
tangled branches, and her stable yet gentle voice telling shimá lessons in
leading a good life. After we finish loading the trucks with firewood, me,
shínaaí, and shiye' Jaiden take our place picking piñons, and we never pick
as much as our mom or grandma, but we try our best. Shimásání smiles as
she picks piñons and in Diné she says *I'm picking these for my little grandson living over the ocean,* and all we can do is return her smile and blink
away tears from missing him. At the end of the day, we return to our home
and gather around shimá's dining table. We share food and memory in the
warmth of shimá's fireplace.

Back at our home, Níłtsą́ Biką' flashes in the west, peaking over the
mesa behind our house before descending into our valley. For what seemed
like hours, lightning flashed white, and water poured from the sky onto
Nihimá Nahasdzáán. Following the lightning were loud bursts of thunder that shook our house, shook my being, and shook the world into silence. When Níłtsą́ Biką' began riding away on his dark horse of deep gray
clouds, lightning flashing from his bow somewhere over Tsoodził's peak
in the southeast, my siblings and I walked to the returned river that ran
from west of our home, down between two mesas, and stretched into the
east. The silence contained frogs croaking their throaty songs and water
rushing over chamisa and various desert brush. This unnamed river, and
for us it was a river with all the magic of rivers, flowed for hours, into the
night and sometimes into the dawn. We stood at its makeshift bank, our
feet covered in plastic bags, pants and jackets soaked, marveling at the
river's movement, its sound, its touch like a cool hand flowing around our
sun-kissed calves and interlacing our earth-brown hands.

After playing with frogs, wading through the current, and splashing each other, we returned home, all the while our plastic-covered feet sunk deep into the mud. Each time we lifted our feet, the mud releasing us sounded like its Diné name hashtłʼish. Tłʼish, tłʼish, tłʼish, tłʼish accompanied the cacophony of frog song and rushing water behind us, and our mom shouting, "Yahanáohjeeh! Get inside! You'll catch a cold!" before us. Once inside, after a fierce scolding that shook us like Níłtsą́ Biką' riding through, we dried off, changed clothes, and sat on the couch swathed in mismatched quilts sewn together by shimásání. Sometimes her smell lingered in the fabric, Avon lotion, and dééh.

Later, as the sun moved west, stretching the mesa's shadow across our valley like an evening blanket, and a crystal-clear moon hung in dusky blue fading into pink, the river's steady rush and the frog's throaty lullaby were constant through our open window. Before bedtime, my mom would give each of us an aspirin so our legs wouldn't ache from the cold pulse of the river. No matter how many layers I wore and despite the aspirin, my legs ached. It was a deep throbbing in my muscle—pain steady like the river's current. The river had entered me somehow, seeped into my muscle, and curled up within. After a slight "I told you so," shimá would massage my legs. Her hands were always warm. She would massage my legs and blow the pain from her hands toward the north. Although the pain from the cold stream subsided, monsoon rains continued to swirl and thrash inside me, somewhere in the darkness of memory, the same interior darkness as the earth's core that cradles my heart, my lungs, and I remember the rain, always the rain over the mesa, over the fields

rain
   rain
      rain
      rain

Rain, Saad, and Land

In Diné thought, rain/moisture is integral to our lives. There are many teachings and stories about rain, and in each, rain is a powerful force with creative and destructive potential that should be respected. Often, rain is characterized as having a female (creative) and male (destructive) essence, as shown in the following poems by Diné poet Laura Tohe, from her collection *Tséyi': Deep in the Rock.*

FEMALE RAIN   MALE RAIN
Female Rain   Male Rain
   Dancing from the south   He comes riding a dark horse
     cloudy cool and grey   angry malevolent cold
      pregnant with rainchild   bringing floods and heavy winds

At dawn she gives birth to a gentle mist   Warrior rain having a 49 night
   flower bow with wet sustenance   Then rides away leaving
     luminescence all around   His enemy behind[1]

Tohe describes Níłtsą́ Bi'ááד using feminine characteristics such as being "pregnant with rainchild" and giving "birth to a gentle mist." This type of rain is gentle with no lightning or thunder. As the rain falls lightly, animals like birds and insects can be seen flitting about from desert brush to desert brush and as the water pools; these animals may even take baths and sing. It is a rejuvenating rain that leaves the earth glistening. The smell of wet earth is engrained in my memory, reappearing when I am traveling and missing home. When Níłtsą́ Bi'ááד brushes her skirt across the land and a full rainbow stretches over the mesa in the east, shimásání likes to step outside and collect the rain in her palm. She blesses herself with the rain, massaging her body with the moisture from her feet up to her head. As children, me and my siblings gathered around her and imitated her smooth movements. Even now, as young adults leaving home for school and work, we remember this teaching and pause in our busy lives to appreciate Níłtsą́ Bi'ááד anywhere we are. But just like shimásání can be gentle one moment and strict the next, the rain also takes on a masculine (destructive) nature in the form of Níłtsą́ Biką'. Tohe describes this rain as a "warrior rain," which brings "floods and heavy winds." Reflected in my recollection above, this rain is characterized by thunder and lightning with flooding. While Níłtsą́ Biką' thrashed about in our valley, shimásání would turn off the television and radio so we could sit in silence. She would say, *Don't lay down and don't stand near windows or doorways. Níłtsą́ Biką' is riding through so we must be quiet and respect his travels.*

Like many things in Diné thought, the rain embodies creation and destruction, both important in the cycle of life.

Reverence for rain appears in works by numerous Diné poets. In the poem "Iridescent Child," Diné poet Nia Francisco illustrates a connection to land, including rain, that is central to Diné thought. Francisco writes:

> My hair black like storm clouds
> and you will often see black birds
>   flying through my thoughts
>   and gestures
>   I am the land and the land
>   is me
> My breath is the rain essence
>   my finger nails are chips of abalone shell
>   and I have a purple shadow
>   like a hedge hog cactus
> and I've been cured
>   by the smoke of cedar bough[2]

More than an inanimate object to be mined for resources, the land in Diné thought is personified, referenced in songs and prayers as Nihimá Nahasdzáán. As children of this earth, Diné are composed of the same natural elements as Nihimá Nahasdzáán with sacred winds in our breath, rain streaked through our hair, and earth that molded our bodies. As Francisco notes, "I am the land and the land is me." In this way, a reciprocal relationship is established in which land itself reflects humanity and humanity reflects the land. Humanity and land become inseparable and indistinguishable from one another. Even in writing this, typing "the land" feels alien. Words like "land," "landscape," "earth," "nature," "the natural world," and any other demarcations of the places we exist in expressed through the English language feel like a separation, like saying this place in which we live exists outside of my own being and isn't related to me like my human relatives. Instead, acknowledging this earth as Nihimá Nahasdzáán and adhering to the Diné maxim k'ézhnídzin, decentralizes human experience and aligns Diné personhood with familial relationships present within all of creation. Francisco's poem, then, rings true—*I am the land and the land is me.*

My breath is rain essence. This line from Francisco's poem emphasizes the importance of human breath, and in extension speech and language. In *The Sacred: Ways of Knowledge, Sources of Life,* Francisco explains, "The breath of mankind is sacred—and so long as the breath is wet, moist, the words that are spoken are sacred and alive."[3] In Diné bizaad, the human breath is often referenced as hayooł, meaning the wind that resides in a person's body. The connection between human breath and wind is explained in Hajíínéí Bahane', in which sacred winds entered the bodies of First Man and First Woman to give them life. From then on, these same sacred winds entered the bodies of newborn babies, as evidenced by the lines on a person's palm and the whorl atop their heads. While wind is present and provides a sense of movement, Francisco posits that rain/moisture is present as well and offers vitality to human breath. In the poem, rain is a rejuvenating and creative force that is aligned with Níłtsą Bi'áád and imbues breath/speech/language with an aliveness that allows for growth and change. Wind and rain are essential elements that imbue breath, and in extension speech/language, with sacredness and aliveness. In this way, human breath/speech/language carry immense responsibility and creative possibility.

This connection between the breath/speech/language and the rain/moisture is also reflected in works by Diné poet and hataałii Rex Lee Jim. In an untitled poem in his collection *saad,* Jim writes:

> saad éí níłtsą át'é
> saad éí łeezh át'é
> saad éí nanise' át'é[4]

Jim relates saad, which translates to "language" or "voice," to the natural elements níłtsą (rain), łeezh (dirt), and nanise' (plants). As the lines continue down the page, there is a progression of growth in which níłtsą falls and nourishes łeezh, which then encourages nanise' to grow. In relating saad to these natural elements, Jim is making the case that saad also can manifest growth. *Saad éí níłtsą át'é.* Language or voice is the rain and has the potential to nourish and the potential to destroy. *Saad éí łeezh át'é.* Language or voice is dirt or earth, which can be a stable foundation from which new life can emerge. *Saad éí nanise' át'é.* Language or voice is plant life, growing with each generation and sustaining human life. In each iteration of saad, an integral connection is established between language or voice and natural elements. This connection situates human breath/language/voice in a reciprocal relationship with Nihimá Nahasdzáán, in which both need the other for survival and growth. As a poet friend of mine once said, *When we read our poems out loud, the trees are happy to listen to what they gave breath to.* Through breath/voice/language, our poems and stories live and breathe in the world as more than lines printed on paper—our poems and stories nurture the land and our people.

I Am the Land and the Land Is Me

A few years ago, at a family gathering, one of my cheiis told family stories I hadn't heard before. Like many family gatherings, whether for ceremony, birthday celebrations, or more tragic events like the loss of a family member, my relatives sat outside and talked. Beneath the shade of a tall green tree my grandparents planted when they were first married, my relatives gathered. There were several trees with deep green leaves clustered together. One of my másánís mentioned once that the place where my family's homestead is located has an even more specific name—T'iis Sikaad. It was a hot day and a few clouds drifted lazily across the brilliant sky. Even shicheii's dogs, who were often energetic and silly, lounged about in the shade, their ears perking up at the faintest sounds—the wind rustling the tree branches; brown birds fluttering between the ground and the tree; horses galloping in the distance.

When I was a child, this gathering of adults signaled "serious talk," and the children stayed away so they could continue playing. Some of my grandparents have passed on since then. Their stories live on in shimá and her siblings. As I grow older, shimá often reminds me to listen when older relatives are talking. "When you see your cheiis and másánís come together to talk, you listen. Listen and really take it in. Stories come into your life for a reason." These days, I focus my complete attention when an older relative speaks. I focus my attention on their stories, their songs, their breaths, and I strive to know why their particular sharing has come across my path. In this way, maybe I, too, can live a life of strength, determination, and joy.

As my cheii stood, he cleared his throat, and everyone's chatter quieted. His stories began with "When I was a young man" or "In days past," all in

Diné bizaad, and the audience was brought into the story with my cheii. In one story, my cheii talked about my old Grandma Mary and how he helped her herd sheep at the base of the mesa. While my cheii would keep a close eye on the sheep atop his horse, my old Grandma Mary would spread a blanket out on the ground and arrange her balls of yarn around her. She would sit on her blanket, spinning her wool, and every so often, she shaded her eyes from the sun to check on my cheii and the sheep. While my cheii didn't describe his mother, my old Grandma Mary, in detail, I imagine an older woman dressed in a matching skirt and blouse, perhaps a deep green blouse and a lighter green skirt, with her silver hair contained beneath a flowered sáanii scarf, and her hands moving in a steady motion, spinning wool, spinning her dreams and hopes into the wool, spinning our lives into existence below that mesa on a hot summer day. Somewhere, in the stories, in my cheii's memory, my old Grandma Mary is there, and I hope she is proud.

At the end of that summer, the family had approximately a thousand sheep but they lost about two hundred in a blizzard later that year. My cheii recalled herding their sheep on the mesa with his brothers when a storm suddenly picked up, and although they rushed to get back home, the storm stranded them. Throughout the night, they kept their fire going and tried to warm the sheep and themselves, but they lost many sheep that winter. After he concluded his stories, my cheii reminded the family about the history of the land that saw my family through harsher times. In my memory, my cheii said something like, "Despite what people say, let them say it. They want to take the land, but they don't even know its history. Right here, this land has a strong life, a strong connection. You stay right here and keep doing what you're doing." Even now, writing this and reflecting on these memories, these stories, I think about my cheii's lesson that the land has a history, a story, and we have a connection to the land through stories and our lived experiences. Several years back, shimá decided to move back to the family homestead to help shicheii and shimásání in their older years. Shimá was the only one of her siblings to remain at the original family homestead. I think my cheii's sentiments were especially salient for shimá and my siblings.

Later that evening, after my relatives left shimásání's home, me and shimá took our usual evening walk down our dirt road toward the east, across the main county road, until we ascended the hills that lead up to Tsé

Chį́į́h Łichíí' Da'azkáni. All the while shimá's dogs followed along. Their furry bodies were quick blurs in the desert brush as they hunted rabbits and prairie dogs. At the top of the hill beside the mesa, the land below fanned out into fields and mesas that surrounded our homestead on all sides. Each mesa held stories and memories; some we would never know. Shimásání referred to this shorter mesa in the east as Tsé Chį́į́h Łichíí' Da'azkáni because of the rocks that simmered a dusky red in the evening light. From her porch, we liked to sit side by side on cool evenings and watch the rocks blush deeper shades of red until it looked as though the horizon was ablaze. Shimásání's memory began dwindling several years back, so moments where she told stories and shared memories from her childhood were even more special. On weekends when shinaaí and shiye' Jaiden returned from Phoenix, we hiked this mesa to a spot where the sand was black and crystals formed naturally in the crown of the mesa. Tucked away in one of the mesa's folds, partially hidden by a cluster of trees, was an old táchééh. Its huddled shape and pile of lava rocks could be glimpsed from our walking trail. Shimásání instructed us to avoid this area, so we never ventured closer. During our walks up the mesa, I wondered about the songs and prayers this mesa heard throughout the years. In the quiet and stillness of the mesa, I imagined the land vibrating with each song, prayer, and story, with each sound unfurling into the desert brush, ant pile, juniper tree, and sand folding in the breath of the hot summer breezes that winged through our valley.

As my cheii said at our family gathering, the land has a history, and we were one strand of that history. While there was much about the land that would remain obscured, my connection to land emanates from growing up with this land and exploring its finer details. Whenever my travels take me away from my homeland, I can imagine the view from atop the mesa in detail, but even more spectacular are the memories of being in the land. I remember the summer rains—shimásání calling the children inside before the storm burst overhead; me and my siblings seated quietly in her small, pink living room with our smiling faces reflected in picture frames scattered in haphazard patterns on the walls; shimásání speaking softly and telling us about our parents and how raucous they were growing up. After the rain had passed, we gathered outside beneath the smaller green trees that grew nearby, and shinaaí or shicheii would shake the tree and the water glistened as it fell all around us, and our laughter rang clear in the muted afternoon calm. We used to squat around a muddy puddle and make mud pies with my sisters. The mud was cool on our hands, blending into our skin. Shimásání and shicheii sat side by side nearby, quiet and smiling. How we thought those summer rains would always come back to us.

I remember climbing the mesas with shinaaí, my cousins, and my uncles to find a camping spot. Back then, we didn't use tents but rather unrolled our blankets on the warm sand. At night, we fell asleep beneath the night's shawl woven from darkness, and Yikáísdáhí's shimmering star body stretched across the horizon. In the early morning, dew settled on each plant and tree, and the birds called out, their songs rising to meet a new day. I remember hauling wood from the nearby mesas. Shicheii drove an old, white Chevy truck; me and shinaaí bounced around in the truck's cab with the windows down, and shicheii drove with one arm out the window and his dark shades reflected our smiling faces. On the mesa's rim, we found a dead tree designated as a "gooder one" because of how big it was and the way it leaned to the side, making it easier to topple. I worried about the flowers and grasses that surrounded the tree like a skirt, but shicheii assured me they would grow back soon and life would continue like that—how I miss shicheii in those rememberings. Somewhere in those memories, shicheii continues to smile and instruct me and my siblings on life. Somewhere in those memories the rain continues to fall and we gather around our favorite tree to shake the water, and our laughter adds to the history of this land, this land that knows us.

Land, Time, and Storytelling

Like many Diné families, we often drove an hour to Gallup, a nearby bordertown dubbed the Indian Capital of the World and Drunktown, to buy groceries and other necessities like drinking water and for the laundry. Driving south from our home toward the I-40, we passed through several designations of land—Navajo trust land, Bureau of Indian Affairs land, and state land. While we couldn't see lines demarcating these distinct land spaces, any map of the Navajo eastern agency resembled a checkerboard, with various designations of land replete with their own rules and regulations. What was apparent was the condition of the road. Once we left Navajo trust land, our dirt road became paved, which we appreciated most during the rainy seasons because pavement meant no muddy roads and no risk of getting stuck. One summer, we drove with my cheii toward Blue Water Lake to gather firewood, and as we passed onto the paved road where the state land began and where white ranchers had settled several years before, shicheii shook his head and remarked, "Bilagáanas don't have to ask twice for anything. Our side of the road gets worse every year." At the time, I didn't pay much attention to this remark. Shicheii often made similar statements during our drives on this road, and each time I wondered what he meant. Now, I realize shicheii had pointed out the non-Diné obsession with mapping and land ownership, in which lands were seen as property and a resource. Within this mapping, bilagáanas made the rules, and my community got the short end of the stick.

For Diné, this sense of mapping isn't innate but rather something learned through colonization. Instead, Diné thought locates the human in relation to the temporal space of Nihimá Nahasdzáán. In an untitled poem printed in *Between Sacred Mountains: Navajo Stories and Lessons from the Land*, Diné poet Tábąąhí Ts'ósí communicates a similar sentiment to Francisco and Jim. He writes:

Nahasdzáán shimá dii'ní.
Bits'ą́ądóó neidá.
T'áá ákwíí jį́ náánihiidlááh nidi
T'áá bí néidleeł.
T'áá éí ániit'é.[5]

Tábąąhí Ts'ósí's poem emphasizes the familial and reciprocal relationship between humanity and Nihimá Nahasdzáán, in which Diné call the earth my mother, and we return to the earth later on in life. In this perspective, human existence isn't the pinnacle of all creation, as portrayed in Western epistemology, but rather humans exist in the natural order of the world as one component, one small piece in the complex tapestry of iiná. Locating oneself within this natural order of the world, or this natural temporal space, reflected in Diné thought, diverts Diné personhood out of hierarchical conceptualizations of time and space. In perceiving our world, the one in which temporal space exists, there is a hierarchy in place that privileges time constructed from the European legacy of colonization. In *What Is a World? On Postcolonial Literature as World Literature*, Pheng Cheah writes: "The subordination of all regions of the globe to Greenwich

Mean Time as the point zero for the synchronization of clocks is a synec-
doche for European colonial domination of the rest of the world because
it enables a mapping that places Europe at the world's center . . . a form of
imprisonment that smothers lived local temporalities."[6]

The time in which we currently operate, including days that are broken
up into twenty-four-hour periods and various time zones, has its roots in
European colonization. This construction of time enforces a European
sense of order that lassos nonwhite bodies, displacing their experiences
of the world and relegating their beliefs to some other field of existence,
one that is now classified as "myth" or not reality. For Diné, experiences of
time are heavily intertwined with cycles of the natural world, which lends
itself to multiple facets of Diné life, like entering a space through a specific
direction, offering up prayers at certain times of day, performing spiritual
ceremonies in specific seasons, how to rest your head during sleep, and so
much more. By living under a European-centered construction of time,
we are disrupting a cycle of life that we believe was laid out for us by the
Diyin Dine'é, who brought us into this current world from four previous
worlds below. Similar to mapping as a tool of colonial empire to quantify
land, European-centered time devalues the human lived experience and
implodes how we exist in the world.

In thinking about constructions of Diné time, I return always to ceremonial songs, prayers, and stories. Tohe includes a sampling of dził biyiin
in her poem "Many Horses." She writes:

> Dził bich'į' yishááł . . . I am approaching the mountain
> Dził bikáá' haashá . . . I am ascending the mountain
> Dził bikáá' naashá . . . I am walking on the mountain
> Dził bąąhdóó 'adaashááh . . . I am descending the mountain
> Dził bits'ąąjį' dah diishááh . . . I am leaving the mountain[7]

Ałk'idáá' jiní, a long time ago, it happened, they say, Talking God and
Home God traveled to each sacred mountain in the four directions. Each
time, their arrival was proceeded by a song that continued as they traveled
up and down each mountain in the four directions. In a storytelling session
during the Hozho'o Hoolne Writing Conference in 2019, Jim spoke on
this story of Talking God and Home God's travels to the sacred mountains

as a pursuit of excellence and reveling in the beauty of life. *Dził* translates to "mountain" in English and connotes strength, a rootedness to the
earth that is unyielding in the face of adversity. Jim noted Talking God
and Home God's ascension up the sacred mountains also represented a
yearning for knowledge, to reach the pinnacle through one's own efforts
with prayer and the body in mind. A song was offered before the journey,
during the journey, returning from the journey, and after the journey was
completed.

The image of these two Holy People walking to the mountain, ascend-
ing the mountain, walking on top of the mountain, descending the mountain, and leaving the mountain also represents time, among other essential
elements. Talking God and Home God began their journey in the east
at Sisnaajini, climbing this mountain's eastern side and then descending,
moving to the mountain's southern side to climb and then descend. They
continued in this fashion until they had climbed and descended the mountain on all sides, from east to south to west to north. In Diné thought, this
cyclical movement is called shábike'ehgo, or according to the sun's travel.
Dr. Andy Nez, former Senior Education Specialist with the Navajo Nation
Department of Diné Education and currently a Council Delegate representing Crystal, Fort Defiance, Red Lake, and Sawmill chapters on the Navajo Nation Council, translates shábike'ehgo as "Shá is sun, like shándiin
(sun light). Bike'ehgo is following."[8] According to shábik'ehgo, humanity
does not dictate time, but rather time is observed from the natural order
of the world, or what can be considered natural law. This sequence of four
following shábik'ehgo is also found in Hajíínéí Bahane', in which the original Diné emerged from four worlds prior to this one. The emergence from
the worlds below is demarcated by four layering of colors including white,
turquoise, yellow, and black, as they are ordered in our present world. Our
journey began in the first world, which was black, and we moved through
the blue, yellow, and white worlds into the present world. This movement
from the bottom to the top is referenced in prayers as shikélátł'ááh dóó
shitsiit'ááhjį', which translates to "from the bottom of my feet to the top
of my head" and references earth to sky movement, and movement from
whatever space is below your feet (which might not be earth) to the space
above you (which could be sky or universe). Similarly, an earth to sky
movement can also be found in the dawn where different layers of light

extend upward. When we pray, we are the embodiment of this movement from the first world to the current world, the embodiment of the layers of light at dawn. There is no separation between the human body and the earth body; we are the same entity.

During our emergence into the present world, movement transitioned from shikélátł'ááh dóó shitsiit'ááhjį' (earth to sky movement) to shábik'ehgo (sunwise movement). While one may think that the earth to sky movement is linear, it is cyclical in that within our movement from the four previous worlds there was also movement in the four directions to meet the sacred colors in each of those worlds. This would convey a cyclical movement that continuously moves upward into the present world. In Diné thought, this cyclical or spiraling movement informs how we pray, how our spiritual ceremonies are organized, various ceremonial songs, how the seasons operate, how we enter a space, how we sleep, our poetics, and so much more. As such, this cyclical movement from below upward exists outside of linear time imposed by European colonizers and speaks to a circular way of thinking, in which Diné worldview does not rely on a hierarchy that places humans at the pinnacle of creation. Instead, Diné worldview positions the human body within the natural world as an interpreter rather than a controller.

Pivotal to the Diné worldview is storytelling, which contains numerous iterations of cyclical time and structures. Diné storytelling is rooted within the same cyclical structure set forth by natural elements like the four sacred mountains, the four seasons, and the four layers of light that make up the dawn. Diné storytelling, then, is closely connected to the natural world via cyclical time that encompasses all things. More than quantifiable space or something to be conquered, the natural world is recognized as Shimá Nahasdzáán and human beings as Nihookáá' Diyin Dine'é. This sense of cyclical time extending from Hajíínéí and kinship with the natural world is reflected in ancestral and contemporary stories by Diné storytellers such as Irvin Morris's *From the Glittering World*. These texts contribute to a cyclical time-space in which Diné storytelling resides within the Diné philosophy, and in extension literary tradition, of Są́'ąh Naagháíi Bik'eh Hózhǫǫn (SNBH). This concept connotes a never-ending cyclical time, in which stories and teachings contribute to a balanced human experience. In his essay "A Moment in My Life," Jim interprets SNBH:

In one poem, I referred to the formula as 'May I be Everlasting and Beautiful Living' . . . *Sạ'ah naagháí bik'eh hózhóón nishłǫ́ǫ́ naasháa doo*. In short, this declaration of a healthy and wealthy lifestyle means to me the beauty of life realized through the application of teachings that work. Literally, *sạ* means old age, *ah* means beyond, *naa* means environment, *ghái* means movement, *bi* means to it, *k'eh* means according, *hó* means self and that sense of an ever-presence of something greater, *zhóón* means beauty, *nishłǫ́ǫ́* means I will be, *naasháa doo* means may I walk. This may be stated in the following way. "May I walk, being the omnipresent beauty created by the one that moves beyond old age."[9]

Jim's interpretation moves beyond sạ (old age) toward zhóón (beauty). This is achieved by way of effective teachings inherited from ancestors. Effective teachings defy death and enrich the human experience. In addition, sạ can also mean humanity, seeing as we are the ones that experience old age and then die. What moves beyond old age to a state of beauty are teachings, which can be interpreted as knowledge. We've inherited knowledge from our ancestors who journeyed through the four sacred worlds to the present; we've inherited knowledge from our ancestors who faced extermination at the hands of the U.S. government; we've inherited knowledge from our ancestors who were forced to attend government boarding schools where our language and way of being was nearly eradicated. We continue to inherit knowledge from literary ancestors who write from their Diné personhood, reaching into the depths of humanity, and offering their knowledge on the page. This movement of knowledge, sprouting from Hajíínéí to the present, mimics the cyclical time movement. As such, our contemporary experiences add to cyclical time that carries our stories into the future. In this way, we move beyond our present experience and travel alongside Talking God and Home God up the mountains and back down again until we reach a state of beauty.

Jim's interpretation also emphasizes a need for stories and teachings carried forth from Hajíínéí in constructing Diné identity. Within Diné storytelling resides a deeper understanding of language and place that transcends colonial notions of writing, authorship, genre, and although not usually considered within this same group, humanity and time. Through the written word, contemporary Diné storytellers contribute to knowledge flowing within cyclical time and, whether consciously or not, write against mapping and time as colonization's tools. Rather than relying on historians and "authorities" on Native American and specifically Diné culture, Diné storytellers are writing their own narratives and giving voice to those that were once silenced. Considering this perspective, the power of Diné storytelling stems from voices present since the beginning of Diné time, their prayers and hopes etched within each word, each line reverberating with the power of SNBH. In her acclaimed book *A Radiant Curve*, Tapahonso writes:

> We
> must remember the worlds
> our ancestors
> traveled.
> Always wear the songs they gave us.
> Remember we are made of prayers.
> Now we leave wrapped in old blankets of love and wisdom[10]

Tapahonso's poem hints at the upward spiral motion of Hajíínéí. However, her poem doesn't begin its meaning making from the bottom moving toward the top. Instead, the poem follows how we would typically read a poem from top to bottom. Tapahonso's poem uses "remembering" as a way of reaching into the worlds below to pull up prayers and "old blankets of love and wisdom." This honoring of the stories, songs, and prayers we've inherited connects us back to the idea of SNBH, in which we are not separate from the experiences of our ancestors. We are connected through the vehicle of story that exists within cyclical time residing within SNBH. Language, in this way, is more than static lines on a page, but an extension, a reverberation, of love and healing from ancestors who imagined us into existence. Language and storytelling connect us across time and place.

Delving deeper into Hajíínéí, additional elements that construct Diné time in relation to the natural world are present. Morris's *From the Glittering World* paints a complex tapestry of Diné personhood. Spanning various genres and forms, Morris's novel is steeped in cultural stories and ideologies and borrows its name from the Diné creation story, in which the Nihokáá' Diyin Dine'é ascend from four previous worlds into the present or Glittering World. The reference to "glittering" is both culturally significant and reminiscent of modern technology, which also glitters and shines. Morris situates the text within ancestral Diné storytelling by beginning with Hajíínéí. Morris writes: *"Alk'idáá' jiní.* It happened a long time ago, they say. In the beginning there was only darkness, with sky above and water below. Then by some mysterious and holy means, sky and water came together. When they touched, that's when everything began."[11] Morris's use of *"Alk'idáá' jiní"* harkens back to ancestral Diné stories and teachings present within SNBH, positioning the text in conversation with Diné origin. The word *"alk'idáá"* glosses to "a long time ago" and suggests a continuation of older stories, contributing to a continuous creation story with no end. The middle part of the word, "k'i," refers to a mountain path, connecting notions of time to the natural world. The word *"jiní"* can be interpreted as "they say" and conveys a sense of communal storytelling, in which the storyteller continuously adds their perspective or voice to the story being told. The "they" is ambiguous but commonly understood to mean ancestors or those that came before us. Taken together as *"Alk'idáá' jiní"* or "It happened a long time ago, they say," this phrase both situates this text within a larger body of oral storytelling and allows room for interpretation, perhaps even variations in the details of the story. In this sense, a non-Diné perspective might bring into question the reliability of the narration, but this phrase adds greater authority to the story because of its ties to the ancestral past and the land. Furthermore, *"Alk'idáá' jiní"* as a storytelling device and a construction of time exists within the same field as the mountain song presented earlier in this work. Time, the natural world, humanity, and the spiritual exist within this field where the mountain looms. While some may view the creation story as "myth" or "folkore," Diné writers revere this story and its elements as sacred history inherited from ancestors. Aesthetically, this phrase also carries sentimental meaning and a variation of analepsis, in which we can imagine countless stories told since the beginning of Diné time using this phrase and adding to its authority, beauty, and power. Morris's work models how to combine Diné cultural stories with a contemporary prose. When doing this kind of writing, it is imperative to respect the ancestral stories. Morris situates the ancestral past in conversation with the contemporary present, even conjecturing that the origin story continues today and that modern technology is our "glittering world."

Morris further emphasizes the idea of language connecting across time by interweaving facets of narrative prose, cultural stories, and history. In writing about the Diné's return from Hwééldi or Fort Sumner, Morris depicts many Diné gaining first sight of Tsoodził, which marks the southern edge of Diné Bikéyah. Upon their return, it has been told that the Diné sang out "*Áhálááneeʼ*" and wept with joy. Morris concludes the chapter "*Náʼiiʼnaʼ* (Comes back to life)" with the following line: "'*Áhálááneeʼ*'!' the people cried. 'We are nearly home!'"[12] In this context, the word "*áhálááneeʼ*" can be interpreted as a form of everlasting or profound love for a place. Within Diné language, there are variations of love, ranging from romantic, to kinship, and finally to the spiritual or profound. Morris follows up this historical chapter with a personal narrative, in which he describes his own view of the Diné homeland in the present: "I can see a wide sweep of my beloved homeland. From there, I am reminded of who I am: I am not alone, nor am I the first. The land has birthed and sustained all my grandmothers and grandfathers. *Áhálááneeʼ*."[13] This passage echoes the previous one through the repetition of "*áhálááneeʼ*" and connects Morris's present experience to that of his ancestors. This term, then, acts similarly to "*alkʼidáá' jiní*" and connects the present to the past. Both terms stitch together moments in time to establish a continuous, everlasting creation story in accordance with SNBH. Morris realizes in this section that contemporary Diné storytellers are not alone, and we continue the cultural legacy of our ancestors within the spiral of cyclical time (or SNBH) in our homeland.

There is no distinction between the past and the present. Diné storytelling and contemporary Diné writing exist within cyclical time as part of SNBH. Through traditional storytelling tropes and devices uttered since the beginning of creation, our stories become the stories of our ancestors and, in turn, we pass on those stories to our children. The function of language within these texts reminds me of Jim's interpretation of SNBH, in which we go beyond old age through effective teachings. We are constantly adding to a body of Diné storytelling that has existed for thousands of years prior to the invasion of our homelands. Through the ideology of SNBH, we are forever connected to our sacred inheritance, and contemporary Diné writers remind us of the power in our words and the possibilities contained within stories.

In the Cornfield

In the summer, early in May, around the time Dilyéhé disappears into the western horizon, me and my brothers plant a garden for nihimá. We till the soil several days before planting: breaking up the harder parts of the soil and mixing in fertilizer. My favorite part is crumbling dirt clumps between my fingers and letting the soil fall through my fingertips. There is something deep about feeling the earth with your hands, a similar feeling to dirt baths after táchééh. It is a feeling of connection, like my body is the same as the earth body and that I am never alone, no matter where I travel, no matter the distance. After we prepare the soil, we plant rows of corn, watermelon, squash, tomatoes, green beans, and onions. Around each planted seed, we create shallow earthen bowls to catch the rainwater. Each row houses these earthen bowls, and after the rain passes through, the rows shimmer and reflect the turquoise sky. Over the next few weeks, we water the plants, talking to the earth and the budding vegetation. Shimá recalls stories of our old Grandma Mary and how she also communicated with the plants.

With few clouds drifting in the sky, heat distorts the fields surrounding our home, turning each desert brush and yellow chamisa into shimmering bodies. Shínaaí waters the garden and shiye' Jaiden walks barefoot through the empty rows between plants. His light brown feet sink into the dark brown mud, and he laughs, enjoying the squishy mud between his toes. Shínaaí sprays some water from the hose into the air, and the rain falls gently around us. Shiye' Jaiden lifts his face and closes his eyes and laughs. His laughter is bright and warm. Shimá sits on a chair nearby, her sun hat shading her face, and she says, "Old Grandma Mary would be proud. Cheii would be proud too." In the shimmering heat of another day in Diné Bikéyah, we gather in the cornfield. Like this, we continue moving forward, with the sound of rain approaching. Like this, we continue moving forward, secure in the knowledge that this land cradles our family and our people in its warm comfort. Through the land, we come to know who we are. Through the land, we become rooted into a humanity that recognizes we are mere beings, a part of a larger system that will continue for all time. But always, the rain and the corn, the corn swaying in fields, everlasting fields of story and memory and love.

IN THE CORNFIELD	DÁ'ÁK'EHDI
in the corn field	dá'ák'ehdi
corn stalks rustle	dá'át'ąą yiigháád
deep green	yéego dootł'izh
with life	'iiná yił
Female Rain glides	Niłtsą Bi'ááд yiilzhoł
from the south	shádi'aah déé
the corn moves about	náádą́ą́ nida'iiná
for the rain	niłtsą bá
an old dance	t'áá nileidéé
from the beginning	'akotao nida'iiná'
tassels gold	'akaz neezt'ao łitso
with corn pollen	tádidiin bee
catch	dá'ák'ehdi
rain	niłtsą 'ayookeed
in the corn field[14]	

Notes

1. Laura Tohe, *Tséyi': Deep in the Rock* (Tucson: University of Arizona Press, 2005).

2. Nia Francisco, *Blue Horses for Navajo Women* (Greenfield: Greenfield Review Press, 1988).

3. Peggy Beck, Anna Lee Walters, and Nia Francisco, eds., *The Sacred: Ways of Knowledge, Sources of Life* (Tsaile: Navajo Community College Press, 1977), 273.

4. Rex Lee Jim, *saad* (Princeton: Princeton Collection of Western Americana, 1995).

5. Tábąąhí Ts'ósí, "Untitled Poem," in *Between Sacred Mountains: Navajo Stories and Lessons from the Land*, ed. Larry Evers et al. (Tucson: Sun Tracks and University of Arizona Press, 1994), 18.

6. Pheng Cheah, *What Is a World? On Postcolonial Literature as World Literature* (Durham: Duke University Press, 2016).

7. Tohe, *Tséyi*, 7.

8. Andy Nez, personal interview, March 19, 2020.

9. Rex Lee Jim, "A Moment in My Life," in *Here First: Autobiographical Essays by Native American Writers*, edited by Arnold Krupat and Brian Swann, pp. 229–246 (New York City: Modern Library, 2000), 229.

10. Luci Tapahonso, *A Radiant Curve* (Tucson: University of Arizona Press, 2008).

11. Irvin Morris, *From the Glittering World* (Norman: University of Oklahoma Press, 1997), 3.

12. Morris, *From the Glittering World*, 30.

13. Morris, *From the Glittering World*, 33.

14. A version of "Dá'ák'ehdi" was published in the *Massachusetts Review*, vol. 61, issue 4, "A Gathering of Native Voices."

E'E'AAH / WEST

Fall on Nihikéyah. Courtesy of Lloyd L. Lee.

CHAPTER 5

Challenges to Diné Bikéyah in 2023

Nihikéyah Bich'ą́ą́h Yéiilti' Doo

SHAWN ATTAKAI[1]

Diyin Diné'e nanhinlá

Dził díí' sinilii diyinii haidiila

"Díí biyi' kééhwonoht'į́įdoo" nihidíiniid

Ne'hosdzáán haidiila

"Díí nihimádoo" nihidíiniid

Yádiłhił haidiila

"Díí nihitaa'doo" nihidíiniid

"Díí át'éego kééhwonot'íidoo"

(The Holy People placed us

They created the four sacred mountains

"This shall be your home," they told us

They created the earth

"This will be your mother," they told us

They created the sky

"This will be your father," they told us

"This is how you will live")

Introduction

Some people say that the Diné Nation is like a Third-World country plagued with social problems such as poverty and alcoholism. The source of most of these problems is the land. The land is held in "reservation trust status." What exactly does that mean? It means that the American government, foreign to the Diné, is holding the Diné and land in captivity. The Diné do not consider themselves separate from the land.

The American stance is that the U.S. government owns the land in what is now the United States, and that the Diné have ceded all their homeland. In 1823, the U.S. Supreme Court announced that the basis of all land holdings in the United States is conquest.[2] The court explained that the American government incorporated into American law the fifteenth-century religious doctrine known as "the Doctrine of Discovery," and this is the basis for the American landholding.[3] Under the doctrine, the Court explained its belief that ownership of Native lands went to Europeans upon discovery, and that Native land rights were reduced to possession and occupancy: "While the different nations of Europe respected the right of the natives as occupants, they asserted the ultimate dominion to be in themselves, and claimed and exercised, as a consequence of this ultimate dominion, a power to grant the soil while yet in possession of the natives. These grants have been understood by all to convey a title to the grantees, subject only to the Indian right of occupancy."[4]

With respect to the Diné in the southwest, Article 9 of the Treaty of 1868 states that the Diné will make the reservation their homeland, and that the Diné relinquish the land outside of the reservation:[5] "In consideration of the advantages and benefits conferred by this treaty, and the many pledges of friendship by the United States, the tribes who are parties to this agreement hereby stipulate that they will relinquish all right to occupy any territory outside their reservation, as herein defined."[6]

As a Diné, it is clear that the Treaty of 1868 is one-sided and the Diné did not understand it. We know this to be true because the Diné did not stay within the 1868 reservation after returning from Fort Sumner. It is plain that the treaty reflects only the American side of the treaty discussion, which is consistent with federal Indian policy as announced in *Johnson v. M'intosh*. The treaty drafters did not incorporate the Diné perspective of the land into the text of the treaty. They very likely did not know that in Diné thought, there are no concepts of owning or ceding land in the same way that Europeans thought about land. On the other hand, Hastiin Dághaa'í (Barboncito), the Diné representative to the treaty discussion in 1868, attempted to explain the traditional Diné perspective of the land. However, Hastiin Dághaa'í's words were not properly acknowledged by the treaty drafters. During the treaty discussion, Hastiin Dághaa'í tried to explain the Diné perspective of the land, about the relationship between the Diné and the land:

"When the Navajos were first created four mountains and four rivers were pointed out to us, inside of which we should live, that was to be our country and was given to us by the first woman of the Navajo tribe. It was told to us by our forefathers, that we were never to move east of the Rio Grande or west of the San Juan rivers . .

That our God when he was created (the woman I spoke of) gave us this piece of land and created it specially for us and gave us the whitest of corn and the best of horses and sheep . . ."[7]

It is important to note that this excerpt from the treaty notes is written in English, which means that these are not the exact words spoken by the Diné representative. It had to be *translated twice.* Furthermore, this Diné perspective was not incorporated into the body of the treaty, where it would have had more importance. Instead, the translation was placed merely in the side notes of the treaty, where the treaty drafters deliberately assigned it less significance.

Considering that the European American goal was to take Native land under fifteenth-century religious doctrine, as enunciated by the U.S. Supreme Court in 1823, it is certain that the Americans intended to deceive the Diné, and that it was premeditated. American leaders purport to proceed in good faith, but 't'óó bizábąąh t'éiyá yee yáłti'' (they only spoke with their lips and not their hearts). Thus there is an argument that the American claim to the homeland of the Diné is based on deception.

This chapter discusses one of the main challenges to the Diné homeland in both the present and the future. The discussion will include how European immigration to Diné Bikéyah and Christian doctrine appears to be the primary reason the Diné Nation is experiencing a myriad of problems today. I will conclude by suggesting how the Diné may respond to the injustices of American conquest and domination, by reconnecting with the traditional Diné understanding of the land.

Original Understanding

Prior to Christopher Columbus's arrival to the New World, the Diné lived between the four sacred mountains, Diné Bikéyah, according to the Holy People's instructions.[8]

The land toward the east extended to Sis Naajiní (Blanca Peak), and southward toward Tówoł (Sangre de Cristo mountain range), and Dził Nááyisii (Sandia Mountain).[9] The Diné oral history describes a series of major ceremonies being held along the Sangre de Cristo mountain range from Colorado into New Mexico.[10]

In the south, Diné resided as far as Noodas'éí Dził (Mogollon Mountains), which is approximately two hundred miles east of present-day Phoenix, Arizona. One western Apache in the 1920s describes a raid upon a Diné camp in the Mogollon Mountains:

> We camped on the east side of a mountain, and from here it is strait to Mo-gollon Mountain. . . . One of our chiefs came and told us to go over to the big black mountain that was there, and go up on top of it to see if we could see any fires that would be Navajo camps. . . .
>
> That night we set out and got pretty close to the smoke but could not see it yet. So, they told us to go up on the mountain there and see if we could see any smoke. When we got up there, we saw a camp right below us and we could see lots of sheep being herded by the camp. This was a Navajo camp all right, and so we went back to the others and told them.[11]

To the west, Diné hogans stretched along the Dook'ooslííd (San Francisco Peak) and north along the Tónits'ósíkooh (Grand Canyon): "Béésh Łigai Atsidii ('Silver Smith'—born near Cameron, Arizona; died in 1939), told of a Navajo Dziłk'ijí Bi'áádjí (Female Mountain Top Ceremony) that was held near Desert View in 1862."[12]

In the north, Diné hogans extended from Dził Bízhi' Ádenii (Henry Mountains), Dził Ashdla'ii (La Sal Mountains), Tó Dootł'izhí (Green River), Dibé Nitsaa (La Plata Mountains), and Dził Łigai (San Juan Mountains).[13]

The center of Diné Bikéyah was a patch of land called Dinétah, around the area between present-day Tóta' (Farmington, New Mexico) and Na'az-ísíto' (Cuba, New Mexico).

European Invasion

In the sixteenth century, Spanish conquistadors immigrated to the Southwest. They tried to take the land for its resources and colonize the Southwest. The Spanish were successful in colonizing the Rio Grande near the

Sangre de Cristo mountain range where the Diné lived along the Rio Grande with other Native Americans. Three centuries of Spanish occupation was enough to pressure the Diné to move westward.

During these three centuries, the English, another group of Europeans, colonized the present-day East Coast United States. Consistent with the discovery doctrine, the English immigrants' goal was to take the land for its resources and colonize the continent. From the fifteenth through seventeenth centuries, the English decimated almost all the Native American societies that occupied the present-day United States. The decimation occurred primarily by disease and invasion warfare. The English immigrants formed the American government and expanded westward across the land. They entered the Diné territory in the Southwest by the 1850s. The Americans found the Spanish fighting with the Diné. The Spanish had managed to push the Diné westward to present-day Chama Valley (near the Jicarilla Apache Reservation today). In describing the Jicarilla Apache territory, one Jicarilla elder remarked in the 1930s: "The western boundary of the Jicarilla was Tierra Armilla and Chama. They wouldn't go past Chama and Tierra Armilla in the mountains. They were afraid of the Navaho then."[14] Therefore, following Spanish occupation around the Rio Grande, the Diné occupied the present-day Carson National Forest and the region west of that.[15]

In 1848, the American military waged war with the Spanish and defeated the Spanish in the Mexican–American War.[16] The American government started a campaign against the Diné. The Diné did not understand why the Americans were fighting them. One Diné leader, Hastiin Jaatł'óół Nineezii (Sarcillos Largos), was frustrated with the Americans:

> Americans! You have a strange cause of war against the Navajos. We have waged war against the New Mexicans for several years. We have plundered their villages and killed many of their people, and made many prisoners. We had just cause for all this. You have lately commenced a war against the same people. You are powerful. You have great guns and many brave soldiers. You have therefore conquered them, the very thing we have been attempting to do for so many years. You now turn upon us for attempting to do what you have done yourselves. We cannot see why you have cause of quarrel with us for fighting the New Mexicans on the west while you do the same thing on the east. Look how matters stand. This is our war. We have more right to

complain of you for interfering in our war, than you have to quarrel with us for continuing a war we had begun long before you got here. If you will act justly, you will allow us to settle our own differences.[17]

The Diné did not understand that the Americans were motivated by religious doctrine to plunder for land. Without explanation, the American army invaded Canyon De Chelly in 1864; killed Diné; destroyed their homes and farms; and forced Diné men, women, and children to go to Fort Defiance. The Americans duped the Diné to go to Fort Defiance for food, when in actuality, the Diné were being guided into a trap.

At Fort Defiance, the Americans did not allow the Diné families to leave and force marched them to a military concentration camp hundreds of miles away from the Diné homeland. This became known as Hwééldi' (Fort Sumner, New Mexico). The Diné were imprisoned for four years at Hwééldi. The journey to the concentration camp and the conditions there were so harsh that hundreds of Diné perished at the cruelty of American hands. One elder reiterates an oral story describing the harsh forced march:

On the journey the Navajos went through all kinds of hardships, like tiredness and having injuries. And, when those things happened, the people would hear gun shots in the rear. But they couldn't do anything about it. They just felt sorry for the ones being shot. Sometimes they would plead with the soldiers to let them go back and do something, but they were refused. This is how the story was told by my ancestors. It was said that those ancestors were on the Long Walk with their daughter, who was pregnant and about to give birth. Somewhere beyond K'aalogii Dził (Butterfly Mountain) on this side of Belin (Belen), as it is called, south of Albuquerque, the daughter got tired and weak and couldn't keep up with the others or go any further because of her condition. So my ancestors asked the Army to hold up for a while and to let the woman give birth. But the soldiers wouldn't do it. They forced my people to move on, saying that they were getting behind the others. The soldiers told the parents that they had to leave their daughter behind. "Your daughter is not going to survive, anyway; sooner or later she is going to die," they said in their own language.

"Go ahead," the daughter said to her parents, "things might come out all right with me." But the poor thing was mistaken, my grandparents used to say. Not long after they had moved on, they heard a gunshot from where they had been a short time ago.

"Maybe we should go back and do something, or at least cover the body with dirt," one of them said.

By that time one of the soldiers came riding up from the direction of the sound. He must have shot her to death. That's the way the story goes.

These Navajos had done nothing wrong. For no reason they had been taken captive and driven to Hwééldi (Fort Sumner). While that was going on, they were told nothing—not even what it was all about and for what reasons. The Army just rounded them up and herded them to the prison camp. Large numbers of Navajos made the journey. Some of them tried to escape. Those who did, and were caught, were shot and killed.[18]

This was the brutality of the Americans guided by the discovery doctrine.

American Control

The Americans forced the Diné, at gunpoint, to enter into the Treaty of 1868. The American soldiers made threats to kill the Diné at the treaty discussion.

There was one thing that isn't mentioned in the White Man's histories. A wooden post was put in the ground, and a big billy goat was hit in the mid-section with a stick so that he struck the post repeatedly with his head and horns. I don't know how long this continued. But, after a while, the brains of the goat came out, and that's when they got through with him. Then the general turned to the Navajos and said, "Nowhere, at no time in the future, whatever you do, don't break this treaty. If you get in trouble with Washington or the U.S. Government again and do the things you should not do, that is what is going to happen to you people." He meant what had happened to the billy goat.[19]

When the Americans coerced the Diné to "agree" to the treaty, the Diné were released back to their homeland.

Through the treaty, the Americans attempted to confine the Diné to a rectangular-shaped reservation around the Chuska Mountains west of Dinétah. However, the Diné unquestionably did not understand the land provision of the treaty, the demarcation lines on the map, and returned to their homelands outside the reservation boundaries identified in the treaty. Instead of confining the Diné to the small treaty reservation, the

American government expanded the original reservation about fourteen times, from 1878 to 1934, by Executive Order to its present size.

> The government said our Reservation was bigger than it really turned
> out to be. In four directions were the sacred mountains—to the east Sis
> Naajíní (Blanca Peak), to the south Tsoodził (Mount Taylor), to the west
> Dook'o'oosłííd (San Francisco Peak) and to the north Dibé Nitsaa (La Plata
> Mountains). Inside these four sacred mountains the Navajos had lived many
> years ago. After their return from Fort Sumner the Reservation set aside
> for them was real small, perhaps like a little way from Tséhootsooí (Fort
> Defiance) up to Dził Łíjiin (Black Mountain) and toward the southeast from
> there. Then, on back north to Tooh (San Juan River), that was the size of the
> land that the Navajos returned to. Their homeland had been much larger,
> but the Diné were told that if they would go by the treaty their Reservation
> would be increased in size.
>
> It has been increased I don't know how many times. Hastii Adiits'a'ii Sání
> (Chee Dodge) said some time ago that it had been added 11 times toward
> the east.[20]

For the Diné, the treaty meant a "peaceful" relationship between the Diné and the Americans. Today, the treaty remains the basis of peace between the Diné and the American government.

American Governance and Suppression

The signing of the treaty marked the beginning of American control and suppression of Diné affairs and way of life. Since the signing of the treaty over a century ago, the American government has extensively attempted to colonize the Diné with laws and policies. After the Diné returned to their homelands, the American government began creating more laws to destroy the Diné way of life, taking control and regulating the Diné, their land, and resources. This is a list of some of the offensive laws and policies conceived and implemented against the Diné after the treaty:

- Removal (1850s to present)—Forcefully removing Diné from different areas of Diné homelands, including all of the land between the Sangre de Cristo mountain range and Dinétah (comprising about half of the traditional Diné territory), the Dinétah district in New Mexico, and the lands surrounding the Hopi villages in the Black Mesa area in Arizona. The Diné were pushed to the western portion of their traditional territory, the land between the four sacred mountains.

- Land ownership (1868 to present)—The American government declaring ownership of Diné Bikéyah, according to the treaty and other American laws based on the discovery doctrine.
- Diné governance subjugation (1860s to present)–After the treaty, the Indian agent imposing elements of American governance into Diné society to subdue traditional Diné governance.
- Boarding school (1880s to present)—Forcefully stripping Diné children away from their families for indoctrination into European language, customs, and habits in military-type residential schools.
- Courts of Indian Offenses (late 1880s to 1959)—The agent forming courts and jails based on European models of criminal justice structures.
- Navajo Council (1923 to present)—The agent directing the formation of the first Navajo Nation Council to accommodate American corporations seeking to extract natural resources (oil and gas) from the land around Shiprock and the Dinétah district.
- Citizenship (1924 to present)—The Diné being granted American citizenship for full gradual assimilation into American society.
- Chapter System (1927 to present)—The agent forming the Diné chapter system for local leadership, today consisting of approximately 110 chapters.
- Sheep reduction and grazing laws (1935 to present)—The agent forcefully destroying a significant portion of the Diné livestock, causing collapse of the Diné economy, and in 1957, full implementation of federal grazing, homesite, and business site lease laws.[21]
- Uranium mining (1940s to present)—The American government, in conjunction with private companies, mining more natural resources (uranium) throughout the Diné reservation, leaving a legacy of unremediated mines throughout the reservation. This caused many Diné to die of cancer and related illnesses. Today, many Diné continue to experience high rates of cancer due to unremediated uranium mines and downwinder sickness.
- Public school mandate (1960s to present)—The continued removing of Diné children away from their families for indoctrination into the

American language, habits, and values in American public schools located on and off the Diné Reservation.

- Navajo-Hopi Relocation (1972 to present)—The federal government's
continued removal of thousands of Diné families from their homelands
in the Black Mesa region to accommodate American corporations seeking to extract natural resources (coal).

After the treaty was signed, the American policy makers lost no time
in starting to take the land and resources away from the Diné and other
Native American tribes. Most of these laws were passed to destroy Native
societies under the federal Indian law and the discovery doctrine. However, some of these laws are specific to the Diné, such as sheep reduction
and Navajo relocation.

Modern Social Issues

More than a century of these inhumane policies has led to the destruction and deterioration of the Diné, their land and way of life. Today some
people say that the Diné is an impoverished Third World country within
the richest nation in the world. There is an overwhelming amount of problems on the Diné Reservation. In no particular order, some of these issues
include:

- No land ownership
- Lack of housing, lack of running water, no electricity
- Unquantified water rights
- High crime, violence, and domestic violence
- High alcoholism and substance abuse
- High poverty, no economic development, high unemployment
- An abandoned grazing economy
- Uninhabitable lands due to continued profuse mining in and around
the reservation, unremediated polluted lands, polluted waters, and
high air pollution
- Mass exodus of young Diné who leave the reservation for education
and employment elsewhere
- Loss of language and culture leading to a loss and confusion of identity
among young Diné

- For those who leave the reservation, oppression in American society as people of color
- Depression, high suicide, and loss of life

The Treaty of 1868 is supposed to be a peace treaty, but in function, the American government, with law and policy, continues to destabilize and gradually and subtly extinguish the Diné and Diné way of life. American laws are destroying the Diné gradually and subtly by creating a myriad of problems that make it difficult to live as a Diné in the modern age, on and off the reservation. Diné identity is being erased, the people are being assimilated to extinguish the Diné claim to land so the European can have more access to Diné land and its resources, according to federal policy and church doctrine. This destruction effort continues into the present because almost all the federal policies continue to operate and remain in effect.

With all these overwhelming problems, what can the Diné do?

Fixing the Diné-American Relationship by Starting with the Treaty

The American government promises that the treaty is supposed to govern the *peaceful* relationship between the Diné and the American government, but it seems like the treaty has just created issues and devastation that cause the Diné and Diné way of life to decline. As a matter of survival for Diné, it is important to return to the treaty because land assertion under the treaty is a major focal point. Although the word "cede" does not specifically appear in Article 2, the treaty provision which creates the reservation, the American government claims that the Diné gave up their homeland to the American government.

However, there is nothing *from the Diné perspective* about any land cessation under the treaty. According to the Diné, the Diné have continuously occupied the area between the four sacred mountains since time immemorial. For the Diné, the treaty is a foreign document known as "Naaltsoos Sání" (the old paper) that represents peace. Today, most of the Diné population is uneducated in terms of Western higher education. They believe in the Diné Bibee Haz'áanii (the Holy People's law) that, by divine right, the land between the four sacred mountains belongs to the

Diné. For example, I asked my grandfather (who is now passed), who only spoke Diné, about the land. I asked him, "Kéiya shą' háí bí? Who owns the land?" He responded:

> "Kéiya nídeisiilbá Hwééldi di. Naakidi nída'ahwojoogą́ą́'yę́ędą́ą́', nihi tseełke' Bilagána yá nidaazbaa'. Íídą́ą́' ałdó' kéiya nídeisiilbá." ("We won our land back at Hwééldi. Then at the Second World War, our Diné men fought for the Americans. We won our land back then also.")[22]

My grandfather, like the generations before him, undoubtedly believed the land belonged to the Diné. My grandfather also raised an interesting point. Among all the races, Native Americans have been in every American conflict since its conception, and more significantly, Native Americans have the highest per capita rate in the United States of volunteering for military service.[23] The Diné are no exception with their exemplary service during the Second World War. The Navajo Code Talkers used their language to develop and implement an unbroken code to help the American government during intense battles to win the war for America in the Pacific. There is a saying that were it not for the Diné Code Talkers, we would be speaking Japanese. Perhaps all the Diné who serve in the American military join the military with the understanding that they are helping protect *their Diné land*. When Diné veterans are asked why they join the American military, they always respond, "To defend my people, my homeland, and my way of life."

One oral Diné story about fighting the Americans when the Europeans invaded Diné Bikéyah in 1862 has described the Diné warrior ethic as follows: "There is a chief. His name is Ch'il Haajiní. They call him Manuelito. He tells us to fight for our land. He really cares about his own people. He wants them all safe. He wants them to be in their own land. Soon I feel like fighting along with them, and that's what we did finally. We started. It's hard to do, but we did it."[24]

My Diné people value serving and protecting, so I volunteered for the Marines, as an infantry rifleman, after graduating from college. I enlisted for the same reason: *To defend my people, my homeland, and my way of life*. At no time did I think I was "protecting only the American way of life, and not the Diné way of life." I raised my hand in the winter of 1995 and formally swore that I am willing *to give up my life* in defense of our way of life. And I meant it. At the time I did not appreciate the gravity of the

moment, but in hindsight, I realize that the enlistment oath is a very significant act of courage that many will not volunteer to do—the willingness
to give up everything for a specific cause. It has a lot to do with self-worth,
ego, and identity. To me, as a Diné, the willingness to risk your life defending your land and Diné people demonstrates what our lands between the
four sacred mountains means to us, what we as Diné veterans represent,
and what being a Diné Nabaahii means.

With this strong warrior ethic, other Diné men and women continue
to volunteer to risk their lives to protect the Diné, Diné way of life, and
Diné Bikéyah. The Diné have not abandoned the home between the four
sacred mountains, and many have made the ultimate sacrifice for the love
of their land. Háshinęę' Shikéyah.

However, when Diné men and women decide to volunteer for the
American military today, there is never any discussion about the American claim that the Diné have given up to the American government their
homeland within the four sacred mountains. The military recruiters who
target young Diné never mention that the American government claims
the land between the four sacred mountains. I was never informed of this
important detail when I signed up with a recruiter in Gallup, New Mexico. Perhaps selective service efforts for Diné should include a qualifier,
a statement that the American government does not recognize the Diné
claim to the land between the four sacred mountains so the young Diné
may make an informed decision as to what exactly they are signing up for
without any mistake or trickery. The current recruiting practice of young
Diné is deceptive.

To illustrate the trickery, in 2009, one Diné veteran, after being dis-
charged from the American military, found out that the American government's stance toward the Diné was at odds with his own reasons for
serving the same government. The Navajo Nation Human Rights Commission published a report in 2012 with a description of the Diné veteran's
reaction. The report states:

> Of significance, on December 17, 2009, the Navajo Nation Human Rights
> Commission received Mr. Johnny Jack's testimony and summarized it as fol-
> lows: Mr. Johnny Jack was disgusted with the US Government for using the
> Navajo language to fight against Japan. His three younger brothers went to
> war with the understanding they were fighting for their land. But when they
> returned, they learned their land was taken away by the same government

that they fought for. For Mr. Jack, it made no sense for Diné children to enlist and fight for a nation that took land from the Navajo people—especially
as first occupants. The commission found Mr. Johnny Jack's testimony similar to other Navajo veterans who were confronted with the same dilemma
upon returning from their military service.[25]

It does make no sense to fight for a country that harms your people and
tries to destroy your tribal Diné nation. While the American government
continues to suppress and eradicate the Diné and Diné way of life with
harmful policies, the Diné volunteer in large numbers to protect America,
while unaware of the American government's treatment of the Diné. To
survive as Diné, it is important to start talking about this unequal relationship between the Diné and America. We need to talk about this injustice
starting with the assertion of land ownership under the 1868 treaty. There
is a need for a treaty land discussion that takes into account the traditional Diné perspective. Because the Diné voice has mostly been silent and
erased, the most important task for the modern Diné is to represent the
Diné ancestors who had no adequate representation at the treaty negotiations with the Americans—a crucial time in the history of our Diné people.

The treaty needs to be revisited because the treaty is obviously onesided. The treaty has been drafted and interpreted by Americans to ignore
the Diné's rightful claim to land between the four sacred mountains. By
definition, a "treaty" is an agreement between two or more independent
nations.[26] However, the Diné perspective has been deliberately left out
of the so-called agreement. If one party is left out of an agreement, then
it fails to be a "contract" or "treaty." The true Diné perspective was left
out of the 1868 treaty for two reasons: (1) the American government was
deceptive and (2) a major communication barrier existed. The true Diné
perspective needs to be incorporated into the treaty for the future generations of Diné to exist, survive, and rightfully claim their place in the world
and in the history of humankind.

Treaty Barrier #1: Conquest under
the Doctrine of Discovery

The American party to the 1868 treaty discussion deliberately left out the
Diné claim to land because it was always the European intention to invade

the American continent and decimate its inhabitants according to federal policy and church doctrine. Law students who study federal Indian law in American law schools learn that all the American laws and policies that oppress Native Americans (including the Treaty of 1868) are based upon the Doctrine of Discovery.

Relatively unknown, the discovery doctrine is a fifteenth-century religious international law founded in the papal bulls (official decrees) of the Roman Catholic Church, which was historically used by some European countries to take, by force and violence, Indigenous lands in America and Africa. In 1823, in a case known as *Johnson v. M'Intosh*, the United States incorporated the doctrine into American law as the basis of American sovereignty, property law, and the foundation of federal Indian law.

The doctrine takes its roots in the European Crusades centuries earlier, which attempted to establish worldwide papal jurisdiction.[27] The doctrine was essentially used as a justification to engage in profound wrongdoing, to steal a whole continent and exterminate people of color. When the first Europeans immigrated to America, the intent was to invade the American continent and decimate the Native People according to their understanding of this church policy. At the first opportunity, the European immigrants organized the American government according to the church doctrine, which they termed as "manifest destiny." In grade school, American children are taught that "it was our manifest destiny to establish the American country," when in actuality, the first European explorers, their sponsors, and settlers were extremely evil to execute the world's worst killing in history. Nowhere in the known history of mankind has a genocide occurred to the magnitude of that committed against Native Americans. Due to the European invasion, and pursuant to church doctrine, *millions* of Native Americans were murdered and land theft occurred from *shore to shore.*[28]

Today there is no accountability for the immense historical harm that has been committed against Native Americans. Instead, the oppression continues; more laws and policies are created to destroy the remnants of Native American tribes. Instead of having true honor and courage, it seems like the intent of American leaders is to keep the shameful history hidden in the dark, and to prevent the current practices against Native Americans from coming into the light.

Today, some church denominations are becoming aware of the medieval doctrine being alive and well in America, and because of the doctrine's inhumanity, some churches are starting to publicly repudiate the doctrine.[29]

Over the past decades, Native Americans have requested that the Roman Catholic Church rescind the doctrine.[30] In *Johnson v. M'Intosh*, the U.S. Supreme Court declared that the discovery doctrine is the cornerstone for American property law and sovereignty, and federal Indian law:

> Discovery is the foundation of title, in European nations, and this overlooks all proprietary rights in the natives. . . . All the proprietary rights of civilized nations on this continent are founded on this principle. The right derived from discovery and conquest, can rest on no other basis; and all existing titles depend on the fundamental title of the crown by discovery. The title of the crown (as representing the nation) passed to the colonists by charters, which were absolute grants of the soil; and it was a first principle in colonial law, that all titles must be derived from the crown.[31]

However, just recently in 2023, the Roman Catholic Church formally rejected the Doctrine of Discovery.[32] The pope contradicted the U.S. Supreme Court's assertion that the discovery doctrine justified the killing of millions of Native Americans for their land:

> The legal concept of "discovery" was debated by colonial powers from the sixteenth century onward and found particular expression in the nineteenth century jurisprudence of courts in several countries, according to which the discovery of lands by settlers granted an exclusive right to extinguish, either by purchase or conquest, the title to or possession of those lands by indigenous peoples. . . . The "doctrine of discovery" is not part of the teaching of the Catholic Church. . . . The Church is also aware that the contents of these documents were manipulated for political purposes by competing colonial powers in order to justify immoral acts against indigenous peoples that were carried out, at times, without opposition from ecclesiastical authorities. It is only just to recognize these errors, acknowledge the terrible effects of the assimilation policies and the pain experienced by indigenous peoples, and ask for pardon. Furthermore, Pope Francis has urged: "Never again can the Christian community allow itself to be infected by the idea that one culture is superior to others, or that it is legitimate to employ ways of coercing others. . . . In no uncertain terms, the Church's magisterium up-

holds the respect due to every human being. The Catholic Church therefore repudiates those concepts that fail to recognize the inherent human rights of indigenous peoples, including what has become known as the legal and political 'doctrine of discovery.'"[33]

The declaration essentially stated that Native peoples should not be deprived of their personal liberty or property, and "should the contrary happen, it shall be null and have no effect."[34] The Roman Catholic Church basically pulled the foundation out from under the United States, essentially saying that the church cannot be used to justify the historical stealing of land from the Native Americans, nor can the church be used to justify the racist destructive federal Indian policies still currently in effect. With respect to the land, the U.S. Supreme Court stated that there can be "no other basis" on which American title can be premised.[35] According to its framers, America is a civilized society because it follows the rule of law.[36] If the only basis for American title under the rule of law has been repudiated by the source of that principle, then American title seems to be illegitimate under its own reasoning. If discovery isn't the basis, there seems to be no foundation for all the racist federal Indian laws and policies currently in place.

For purposes of this chapter, the true Diné perspective of land between the four sacred mountains was deliberately left out of the 1868 treaty, partly due to the fallacy of conquest under the discovery doctrine. Finally, the discovery doctrine being the historical guiding principle for the first European immigrants and settlers in America suggests that American leaders did not intend to negotiate the 1868 treaty in good faith with the Diné.[37] Under American law, good faith is understood to be a basic requirement to a contract, which a treaty is. Without good faith, and without a valid legal basis, the treaty purporting to strip Diné people of their land does not appear to be valid.

Treaty Barrier #2: Communication Barrier

Another reason the Diné perspective was left out of the 1868 treaty was because of a major communication barrier between the parties to the treaty. To say that the Diné worldview is different than the European American worldview is an understatement. The two races came from opposite sides of the globe. Their viewpoints are polar opposites, which were vastly different back in 1868 and remain fundamentally different today, except that today, there are bilingual Diné who can better articulate for the non-Diné speakers the differences in the English language. The barrier created by these differences, between the two groups, contributed to the Diné perspective being left out of the treaty.

To help understand how the Diné worldview is different from the American perspective, it may help to compare how the two groups perceive different aspects of life and society, in areas of communication, personhood, land, law, and governance.

Communication

Language shapes worldview. At the time of the treaty discussion, the Spanish had been in contact with the Diné for a couple of centuries, and contact with Americans was fairly new for the Diné. The parties had no idea of each other's language, customs, manners, and way of life. There were people who were bilingual in Diné and Spanish, and there were people who were bilingual in English and Spanish, but during the treaty discussion, nobody was bilingual in Diné and English. Therefore, when the parties to the treaty tried to communicate, each was entirely foreign to the other, and the treaty communication had to occur through a system consisting of three languages (from Diné to Spanish, Spanish to English, and back).

Finally, a United States Army general arrived from the east (or Washington), and the treaty began to take shape. On one side sat the general or haskee-jinaat'áá (war chief) and beside him a White Man who spoke Mexican and English. Beside the White Man sat a Navajo by the name of Ts'oosí (Tsosie) who spoke Mexican and Diné. At the end of the line sat Hastiin Dághaa'í (Mr. Mustache), the man also known as Barboncito. When the general spoke it would be to the man who spoke English and Mexican. He would translate in Mexican to Ts'oosí, who understood that language; and Ts'oosí would translate in the Diné language to Hastiin Dághaa'í.

Then Mr. Mustache would answer in the Navajo language to Ts'oosí, and Ts'oosí would translate in Mexican to the White Man, who would translate to the general in English. There was no time for the Diné to talk to each other. That was how the treaty was made in 1868—about one hundred and four years ago.[38]

Too much meaning was lost through this system of translation, contributing to the Diné perspective of the land being deliberately left out of the treaty. As for the first Diné bilingual in the Diné and English languages, there is a story: "It was decided by some white leaders that two little boys, Chee Dodge and Chááłátsoh (Big Charley), should learn to read, write and speak the English language. The two boys began their lessons with an elderly white man for a teacher, and this continued for two years. At the end of that time, the two boys could understand the language well enough to help in interpreting between the Navajos and the White Men."[39]

Another fundamental difference between the Diné and the Americans was the use of writing to memorialize agreements. Diné is an oral language. American communication occurs in the English language, which is both oral and written. For the Diné, the practice of writing words on paper was an unfamiliar concept. Everything about the writing system was foreign to the Diné in 1868. The concept of a written alphabet, how letters make sounds and words, how words make sentences, and how sentences make paragraphs and ideas were all alien. The Diné did have a writing system in 1868, but it was not on paper based on an alphabet of letters that create sounds, similar to the Cherokee alphabet. The Diné writing system is a system of symbols that carry ideas. This writing system continues to be used by ceremonial practitioners. For the 1868 treaty, American leaders claim that when the Diné leaders put their "X" mark on the treaty document, the Diné ceded their homeland.

The treaty was also drafted in the English language, which is a European language, and for the Diné, it was entirely foreign. As previously mentioned, the Diné had no idea of American nor English language, customs, manners, and way of life.

The Diné were also not familiar with how the writing system was used. The Diné did not know of the practice of putting agreements in writing to memorialize ideas on paper to prevent deception about the agreement. To the Diné, words are sacred. Diné treated promises as sacred. The Diné writing system was also not used in an adverse manner against others. The Diné writing system was used for healing purposes.

Personhood

The Diné focus on being in harmony with the natural environment. Diné address living beings as relatives, with kinship. For example, a Diné may say, "shitsilí" ("my younger brother"). Americans address people by name. For instance, an American may call her brother "James." Further, the discovery doctrine influenced Americans to view Diné, who were non-Christian, as inferior. For example, the American Declaration of Independence still refers to Native Americans as "merciless Indian savages," an offensive label.[40] These racist terms need to be changed, if at all possible.

Land

The Diné view themselves as a part of the land, a living entity who the Diné refer to as "Nahasdzáán Shimá" (Mother Earth). The Diné believe that they *belong* to Mother Earth, and therefore they are inseparable from the earth. The identity of the Diné guides them to remain on the surface of the earth and not to dig into it or go into space. These are some of the fundamental laws. The Americans perceive the land apart from themselves, scientifically, as an inanimate part of the environment. This viewpoint is based on the acquisition of material wealth; thus Americans regard the land as property or chattel, something that can be bought, sold, and owned, to get wealthy off of. At the treaty discussion, Diné leaders did not know that the Americans were guided by the discovery doctrine in their intention to take the land. American leaders did not understand the Diné leader's remark about the four sacred mountains, and that the land cannot be separated from the Diné.

Law

Under the Diné view, the law is alive, it is a spiritual and divine entity, and is a gift from the Holy People. The purpose of the law is to achieve balance in all things. There are consequences for not following the Holy People's law. Under the American perspective, the law is manipulated to control others, to obtain and maintain wealth and power. During the treaty discussion, the Diné leaders did not understand that American laws are man-made, fluid, negotiable, and the American guiding principle was to take the land based on a centuries-old doctrine. The Americans did not know that for the Diné, the law is static and nonnegotiable, especially when the Diné leader explained the Diné guiding principle was to return and live peacefully within the four sacred mountains. The major misunderstanding was that the Diné believed they cannot alienate the land, while the Americans thought they were negotiating for the land.

Governance

Diné leadership is not concentrated in one person or entity; it is not based on coercing others into what to do but is based on influence. People are free to follow or leave a person's leadership. American leadership is centralized in one entity and is based on coercive power. Leaders could, and often do, compel their will on others, its citizens, and tell them what to do. At the treaty discussion, Diné leaders did not understand the centralized power of the American government, that such power was intended to extend over the whole country, nor that the American goal was to use that power to subdue the Diné pursuant to religious doctrine. The American leaders failed to see that Diné leadership was not under one leader but was spread through many local leaders.

One important aspect of Diné governance included the Hozhǫǫjí Nahat'á (Peace Leadership). One duty of Hozhǫǫjí Nahat'á was to resolve disputes within the tribe and sometimes resolve disputes outside of the tribe, with other tribal nations, using elaborate formats and procedures. Some of this traditional Diné governance survives in the Navajo Peacemaking Program today. The Diné peacemaking format involved the acknowledgment of k'é (kinship) between the parties, the use of tobacco, a wise elder who could review the relevant principles to resolve the issue, and the free discussion of all those involved in the matter. Modern Diné peacemaking derives from this tradition.

When the treaty meeting occurred between the Diné and American leaders, the Diné treated the treaty meeting as a peacemaking session, which the Diné were familiar with. Although there is no mention of tobacco, Hastiin Dághaa'í clearly tried to play the role of the elder who recited the relevant Diné law regarding Diné Bikéyah (the story about the God who pointed out the four mountains and four rivers to the Diné mentioned in the treaty sidenotes). Two critical elements were also missing: the practice of k'é between the parties, and the free discussion of all those involved in the matter.[41] In the Diné view, k'é is the foundation of the Diné way of life. The acknowledgment and practice of k'é is the foundation of the Diné peacemaking process. Without a doubt, Hastiin Dághaa'í attempted to practice k'é when talking to the American leader by referring to him as "mother," "father," "spirit," and "as a god."

> If we are taken back to our country, we will call you our father and mother, if you should only tie a goat there we would all live off it, all of the same opinion.
>
> I am speaking for the whole tribe, for their animals from the horse to the dog, also the unborn, all that you have heard now is the truth and is the opinion of the whole tribe. It appears to me that the General commands the whole thing as a god. I hope therefore he will do all he can for the Indian, this hope goes in at my feet and out at my mouth. I am speaking to you (General Sherman) now as if I was speaking to a spirit and I wish you to tell me when you are going to take us to our own country.[42]

Sadly, the American leader's objective was to take Diné land according to federal Indian policy, and the Doctrine of Discovery. In the treaty discussion, General Sherman remains steadfast to taking the Diné homeland by referring to the land boundaries.

From the Diné perspective, the Diné expected the treaty discussions with the Americans to be like a peacemaking session, which the Diné were familiar with. However, all the primary elements of Diné peacemaking were missing. There was no wise elder who could review the relevant principles to resolve the issue, there was no real discussion surrounding the relevant Diné fundamental laws, nor any free discussion by the relevant parties, and most significant, there was American trickery to take the land.

After comparing the two perspectives in different areas (communication, personhood, land, law, and governance), it is unmistakable, and important to understand, that the Diné and Americans have very dissimilar viewpoints and values at a fundamental level. The Diné value relationships and being in balance and living in harmony with the world in a system of equality with all living beings. On the other hand, Americans value material wealth, power, control, and dominance in a hierarchical system. These differences were probably not well-understood at the time of the treaty discussions. Therefore, the wide barrier created by these differences be-tween the two groups, contributed to the Diné perspective being left out of the treaty.

Finally, under American law, a contract (which a treaty is) requires a meeting of the minds.[43] There was probably no meeting of the minds be-cause the Diné perspective was vastly different than the American world-view. Without a meeting of the minds, the treaty, purporting to extinguish the Navajo right to land, appears invalid.

In summary, these two problems, deception under the discovery the-ory and the vastly different worldviews, prevented the Diné perspective of the land from being meaningfully incorporated into the treaty. There was no agreement. The document we call the "treaty" is a reflection of the one-sided terms of what the Americans wanted. Coercing someone by force and threats, at gunpoint, is called "duress," which also invalidates an agreement under American contract law.[44] Therefore I think it is time and *critical* that our educated Diné scholars advocate for our true Diné stance regarding the land between our four sacred mountains.

Conclusion

For the European perspective, the United States represents a power-ful nation purportedly based on freedom, opportunity, and economic wealth. However, for the Diné, the United States represents the aftermath of a terrifying genocide against the Indigenous peoples of the Amer-ican continent that just occurred. Because Europeans have destroyed most Indigenous societies and communities that lived in America, Na-tive Americans today only represent about 2.9 percent of the American population.[45] For the most part, the horrible and dark American history presented in this chapter has been swept under the rug, buried, and erased. As a result, the majority of Americans are unaware of the geno-cide against Native Americans that lingers on currently in the twenty-first century. The majority of the American population is not aware of all of the American laws and policies that continue to destroy Native people in America, nor that such laws are based on a religious doctrine that American leaders refuse to nullify. Native Americans realize that the principles underlying the founding of America can only be described with words such as "immoral" and "evil."

As something to consider, one medicine practitioner from the early nineteenth century described the nature of evil from the Diné perspective and provided a response to such immorality.

"You are made of beautiful things inside," he said. "But you can turn all of the beautiful things to ugly, mean things if you do not try to keep them beautiful. If you allow yourselves to become angry and think evil thoughts, it will soon poison you so that you can no longer find the path of light. You will soon be like a tree that has stood in stagnant water until the insides of its roots turn black and soft. From this day on, you must try to keep your thoughts on the straight path ahead and not look for evil and feel discontented."[46]

Some Americans, like those in government and in the extractive industries, continue to scheme against the Diné homeland and other reservations for more exploitation of natural resources. They do not care about the people. For Native American people, that is the situation.

With respect to the land, there is a profound Native American response. "When the blood in your veins returns to the sea, and the earth in your bones returns to the ground, perhaps then you will remember that this land does not belong to you, it is you who belong to this land."[47]

For Native Americans, the Diné and most other Native American tribes are in a disarray of problems today, being perpetuated by the American government by law and policy. When the Diné nation entered into the treaty, the Diné leaders thought they were agreeing to peace, but this does not look like peace. Being subject to uranium-infested waters, and having your people's culture and language devastated by "education," is not peace. Being destroyed within a nation, like a husband beats up his wife in an abusive relationship, is not peace. That is the predicament.

As Diné, what can we do? My grandfather's words resonate with me when I consider this question, "What can we do?" One time, I was getting a ceremony and my grandfather scolded me with the following words:

"Adéénílnjjh! Háisha' ínt'į? Adéénílnjjh! Dahíndaah." (Remember who you are! Who are you? Remember who you are! Take your place.)[48]

In my opinion, the best solution lies in *remembering who we are*, as Diné. We must remember our Bee Haz'áanii, which instructs that we are one with the land. Through ceremony, the Diyin Dine'é awaken in us that we are the children of the Holy People, ba'áłchíní niidlį. We are one with our Mother. Without mistake, the Diyin Dine'é placed us Diné here between Sis Naajiní, Tsoodził, Dook'o'oosłííd, and Dibé Nitsaa. They instructed us that this is our home and that we are to live and remain here forever. These are our Bee Haz'áanii, which cannot be changed by any human. We have lived here since time immemorial and we continue to walk on this land. We continue to make pilgrimages to our sacred mountains, even those which are located outside the four sacred mountains. The earth and the mountains know us. Therefore, American laws cannot change our relationship with Nahasdzáán Shimá. The American jurisprudence recognizes that people can believe whatever they want to believe.[49] We must continue to uphold our warrior ethic. In doing so, we must continue to advocate for equity and justice as Diné. *Diné do matter.*

Notes

1. J.D., Arizona State University College of Law (2000); B.A., Dartmouth College (1995); Traditional Diné Practitioner (2005); peacetime military veteran (1996). I would like to thank Dr. Lloyd L. Lee for giving me this opportunity to respond to the question, "What challenges does Nihikéyah/Navajo lands face in the coming generations?" I hope this is a stepping piece from which others may learn from and continue advocating for peace, equity, and dignity for Diné, and all other Native nations. We are in an era where the Diné language, teachings, and culture are becoming endangered due to the ongoing assimilation policies of public school and the media. I offer my perspective which is based on my understanding of the Diné way of life. I try to include quotes by some of my mentors, and an understanding of those important words uttered by our Chei Sání, Hastiin Dághaa'í, at the treaty discussion of 1868. With this, I hope that our Diné survive as Diné, with Diné language and culture, into the next millennium. Ahéhee'!

2. *Johnson v. M'intosh*, 21 U.S. 543 (1823).

3. *Johnson*, 21 U.S. 543 (1823).

4. *Johnson*, 21 U.S. 543 (1823).

5. For the land within the reservation, there is no express language in the treaty that the Diné ceded their land.

6. There was only one tribe to the 1868 treaty—the Diné Nation. The word "tribes" (plural) in the treaty suggests that this is a boilerplate treaty term that was not corrected. The American government engaged in standardized boilerplate agreements as a part of a criminal syndicate, the scheme to take land from Native Americans. It is "criminal" because it involves mass genocide that is unlawful under International Law; "Treaty Between the United States of America and the Navajo

Tribe of Indians," concluded June 1, 1868, https://courts.navajo-nsn.gov/Treaty 1868.htm#article2.

7. The four mountains identified by Hastiin Dághaa'í at the treaty discussion in 1868: Sisnaajiní (Mount Blanca of the Sangre de Cristo mountain range near Alamosa, Colorado), Tsoodził (Mount Taylor of the San Mateo mountains near Grants, New Mexico), Dook'oosłííd (Mount Humphreys of the San Francisco Peaks near Flagstaff, Arizona), and Dibé Nitsa (Mount Hesperus of the La Plata mountain range near Durango, Colorado); Berard Michaelis, "Navajo Treaty of 1868: Treaty Between the United States of American and the Navajo Tribe of Indians" (Flagstaff: Native Child Dinétah, 2014), 16.

8. The Holy People's instructions are considered "Diné Bibeehaz'áanii" (a.k.a. Fundamental Law of Diné) and is common knowledge to the Diné.

9. Howard W. Gorman, *Navajo Stories of the Long Walk Period* (Tsaile: Navajo Community College Press, 1973), 41.

10. Hosteen Klah, *Myth of Mountain Chant* (Albuquerque: Valliant Printing Company, 1951), 5–8.

11. Palmor Valor, *Western Apache Raiding and Warfare from the Notes of Grenville Goodwin* (Tucson: University of Arizona Press, 1971), 53–56.

12. Laurance Linford, *Navajo Places, History, Legend, Landscape* (Salt Lake City: University of Utah Press, 2000), 84.

13. Howard W. Gorman, *Navajo Stories of the Long Walk Period* (Tsaile: Navajo Community College Press, 1973), 41.

14. Jicarilla Apache elder interview, interview by Morris Opler, circa 1932, notes on fieldwork with Jicarilla Apache Reservation, Morris Opler Papers 1918–1997, Cornell University Library, Ithaca, N.Y.

15. The Diné oral history describes the Tł'éé'jí being performed along the Canjilon mountain range in New Mexico. Some of the Diné gods are said to reside in the canyon northward toward the San Juan Mountains.

16. The Mexican-American War resulted in the Gadsden Purchase and Treaty of Guadalupe Hidalgo of 1850 where the American government bought the land of the Southwest, which includes the Diné territory. No payment was made to the Diné because the Europeans did not recognize the Diné as a people under the Doctrine of Discovery, which was formally adopted by the American government almost three decades earlier in 1823.

17. David Brugge, *Zarcillos Largos—Courageous Advocate of Peace* (Window Rock: Research Section Navajo Parks and Recreation, 1970), 2.

18. Mr. Gorman relays his grandparents' story in 1973. Even at that time, the Diné were not aware of the goals of federal Indian law and policy, and how its foundation is a religious doctrine designed to steal land by genocide; Howard W. Gorman, *Navajo Stories of the Long Walk Period* (Tsaile: Navajo Community College Press, 1973), 30–31.

19. Gorman, *Navajo*, 38.

20. Gorman, *Navajo*, 40–41.

21. 25 C.F.R. 167 (1957).

22. Hashk'aan Yázhí (Mr. Little Banana), face-to-face conversation, circa 2005.

23. Danielle Desimone, "A History of Military Service: Native Americans in the U.S. Military Yesterday and Today," USO, November 8, 2021, http://www.uso.org /stories/2914-a-history-of-military-service-native-americans-in-the-u-s-military -yesterday-and-today.

24. Tiana Bighorse, *Bighorse the Warrior* (Tucson: University of Arizona Press, 1990), 13.

25. The Navajo Nation Human Rights Commission, *2012 Public Hearing Report: The Impact of the Navajo-Hopi Land Settlement Act Of 1974, P.L. 93–531, et al.* (Window Rock: July 2012), https://nnhrc.navajo-nsn.gov/docs/NewsRptResolution /070612_The_Impact_of_the_Navajo-Hopi_Land_Settlement_Act_of_1974.pdf.

26. *Black's Law Dictionary, 4th Ed.*, s.v. "treaty (*n.*)," accessed October 1, 2022, https//:www.academia.edu/85435991/BLACKS_LAW_DICTIONARY_REVISED _FOURTH_EDITION.

27. Indigenous Values Initiative, "Presbyterian Church (USA) Repudiates the Doctrine of Discovery," *Doctrine of Discovery Project* (27 July 2018), https://doctrineof discovery.org/presbyterian-church-usa-repudiates-the-doctrine-of-discovery/.

28. In 1823, the American government acknowledged that conquest, under the Doctrine of Discovery, is the root of title to every parcel of land claimed by the American government from Native Americans. *Johnson v. M'Intosh*, 21 U.S. 543, 573 (1823). The Supreme Court laid the church doctrine as the foundation to American property and sovereignty; K-Sue Park, "Conquest and Slavery in the Property Law Course: Notes for Teachers," Georgetown Law Faculty Publications and Other Works 2298 (2020): 8–17. https://scholarship.law.georgetown .edu/facpub/2298/.

29. In 2009, upon learning of the Doctrine of Discovery, some American churches have repudiated the doctrine as "evil." For example, "To repudiate explicitly and clearly the European-derived doctrine of discovery as an example of the 'improper mixing of the power of the church and the power of the sword' (Augsburg Confession, Article XXVIII, Latin text), and to acknowledge and repent from this church's complicity in the evils of colonialism in the Americas, which continue to harm tribal governments and individual tribal members"; Evangelical Lutheran Church in America, Repudiation of the Doctrine of Discovery: Social Policy Resolution, CA16.02.04, https://download.elca.org/ELCA%20Resource %20Repository/Repudiation_Doctrine_of_DiscoverySPR16.pdf?_ga=2.1456 39348.148271693.1664958113-522430488.1664958113.

30. Mark Gollom, "Why Pope Francis May Be Hesitant to Rescind the Doctrine of Discovery," *CBC News*, July 30, 2020, https://www.cbc.ca/news/canada/pope -francis-doctrine-discovery-indigenous-1.6536174.

31. *Johnson*, 21 U.S. 543 (1823).

32. Dicateries for Culture and Education and for Promoting Intergral Human Development, Joint Statement of the Dicateries for Culture and Education and for Promoting Intergral Human Development on the "Doctrine of Discovery"

30.03.2023 (2023), accessed April 9, 2023, https://press.vatican.va/content/sala stampa/it/bollettino/pubblico/2023/03/30/0238/00515.html.

33. Joint Statement "Doctrine of Discovery" 30.03.2023.

34. Joint Statement "Doctrine of Discovery" 30.03.2023,

35. *Johnson*, 21 U.S. 543 (1823).

36. *Johnson*, 21 U.S. 543 (1823).

37. "The doctrine of utmost good faith, also known by its Latin name 'uberrimae fidei,' is a legal doctrine of contracts that requires contracting parties to act with honesty and not mislead or withhold information essential to the contract"; All Answers Ltd., "Principle of 'Good Faith' in Contract Negotiations," *Lawteacher.net*, accessed October 1, 2022, https://www.lawteacher.net/free-law-essays/contract -law/good-faith-in-contract-negotiations-3632.php?vref=1.

38. Howard W. Gorman, in Broderick H. Johnson, ed., *Navajo Stories of the Long Walk Period* (Tsaile: Navajo Community College Press, 1973), 38.

39. Rita Wheeler, in Johnson, *Navajo Stories of the Long Walk Period*, 84.

40. Thomas Jefferson et al., Copy of Declaration of Independence. July 4, 1776.

41. The absence of free discussion by all parties involved is what Mr. Gorman was referring to when he said, "There was no time for the Diné to talk to each other."

42. Berard Michaelis, "Navajo Treaty of 1868: Treaty Between the United States of American and the Navajo Tribe of Indians" (Flagstaff: Native Child Dinétah, 2014), 16.

43. A contract is founded upon a meeting of the minds. *Baltimore & Ohio Railroad Co. v. United States*, 261 U.S. 592 (1923). https://www.academia.edu/85435991 /BLACKS_LAW_DICTIONARY_REVISED_FOURTH_EDITION.

44. Under contract law, the definition of "duress" includes "unlawful constraint," "imprisonment," "threats of . . . great physical injury or death." *Black's Law Dictionary*, 4th ed. s.v. "duress (*n.*)," accessed October 1, 2022, https://www.academia.edu /85435991/BLACKS_LAW_DICTIONARY_REVISED_FOURTH_EDITION.

45. Nicole Chavez, "Why the Jump in the Native American Population May Be One of the Hardest to Explain," CNN, October 1, 2022, https://www.cnn.com/2021 /08/19/us/census-native-americans-rise-population/index.html.

46. Wolfkiller (recorded by Louisa Wade Wetherill), *Wolfkiller, Wisdom from a Nineteenth Century Navajo Shepherd* (Layton: Gibbs Smith, 2007), 13.

47. "Native American Proverb," *Ancient Origins*, accessed October 1, 2022, https:// www.ancient-origins.net/history-ancient-traditions/glimpse-intuitive-medicine -native-american-tradition-008157.

48. Eddie Benally, face-to-face conversation, circa 2007.

49. *Reynolds v. United States*, 98 U.S. 145 (1878).

CHAPTER 6

Rethinking Nihikéyah Consciousness

Defying Lateral Animosities and Bureaucratic Mazes of Homesite Lease Living

WENDY SHELLY GREYEYES

Colonized statements invoking lateral animosities and institutional violence are not an unknown phenomenon for many Navajos who have left the homeland for economic opportunities and education. The decision to leave Nihikéyah is not an easy choice. It is a traumatizing negotiation in which Navajos must weigh the reality of the lack of available affordable housing. To enter the process of homesite leasing, requiring a tremendous amount of money, along with setting up water and electricity, roads, and finally the actual home, is dispiriting for many. Many times, the options are to get a *home loan*, but impoverished communities do not have the credit scores to qualify for home loans. Many Navajos have left the reservation for employment, education, and affordable homes. Although the Navajo Nation has opportunities and has pleaded for educated Navajos to return, there are very few jobs permitting them to meet the demands of the high cost of education, student loans, homesite mortgages, vehicle payments and maintenance, gas, groceries, and household bills. The idea of owning a home on the reservation is a pipe dream due to the lack of affordable housing. Homes built on homesite leases have conditions that restrict certain ways the land can be used, the type of structure established, and home ownership of property providing families with equity to accrue some wealth. Presently, homesite leases do not offer the same benefits of financial security imperative for establishing credit. Instead, the Navajo Nation continues to oversee ownership of land, and occupants are restricted to seventy-five-year leases and one lease per person. If water or electricity isn't available, the owner must pay to have water lines and electrical systems installed. If not, then the owner must build outhouses and haul water from local wells or Navajo Tribal Utility Authority (NTUA) locations. These are some of the homebuilding challenges confronting Navajos. *The issue, though, is the entire homesite lease structure deprives Navajo people of wealth.* The experience of deep intergenerational poverty is reflected in the fact that families cannot sell their homes or property. This places Navajos at a disadvantage in entering the home market.

The rest of this section is an analysis of the lived experience of obtaining a Navajo Nation homesite lease. I share the steps described on the Navajo Nation land department homesite lease application and my own personal documents.[1]

Steps to Obtain a Homesite Lease (HSL)

1. Application: Client shall pick up an HSL Application from Agency Land offices or online.
   a. Client will complete Page 2 (Acknowledgment), Page 3 (Joint Applicant Form—if applicable), and Page 4, Section 1.
   b. Client will then meet with a Grazing Officer to record the Proposed Homesite GPS coordinates to complete Page 4, Section 2.
   c. The Grazing Officer will also complete Page 5, Sections 1–3 on Page 5 to distinguish grazing permittee(s) affected within a ½ mile radius of the Proposed Homesite for their consent.
   d. Client then will meet with each grazing permit holder(s) to get their consent, if the grazing permittee consents to your Proposed Homesite Lease, they will sign Page 6 and the Grazing Officer will acknowledge the consent form.

The first step of my homesite lease experience began on August 4, 2014. I started by gathering signatures from the grazing permittees, which consisted of my family members living in the Tsegi area, which is approximately thirteen miles west of Kayenta. This area falls within Navajo County alongside Tsegi Canyon. My father had selected the site, and we began the effort of visiting my family to gather signatures. This took a few months as family members were in and out. At times, my father was the only one to visit family. We finally obtained the six signatures and the grazing official's signature to complete the first part of our application and submitted on October 6, 2014, to the grazing official, Jonathan D. Nez (not the 2018–2022 Navajo Nation president). In the remarks on my application, the grazing official writes, "Wendy?" in big letters at the bottom of the signature page. My signature is not legible, but the application does show my full printed name and address.[2]

2. Submit Application & Fee Payments:
   a. Client should submit the Homesite Leases Application once you get the consent from the Grazing Officer and Grazing Permittee(s), with a money order of $30.00 for the Application Fee, made payable to the "Navajo Nation." (Non-Refundable)

This second step involved acquiring a money order. We went to Bashas's in Kayenta and had the money order issued for $30.00 payable to the Navajo Nation. Following this, we took the forms to Tuba City, Arizona, to the first Navajo land office specialist, Mr. Jarrod Yazzie. He reviewed the six signatures and grazing official's signature. From there, we were told to pull together the next items on the Homesite Lease Checklist.[3]

3. Navajo Fish & Wildlife Department:
   a. Navajo Nation Department of Fish & Wildlife will conduct a Biological Review of the Proposed Homesite. The Biological Request Form will be submitted to the Department of Fish & Wildlife electronically from the Homesite Lease Office. However, the client is responsible for submitting their payment to the main Fish & Wildlife Office by mail (P.O. Box 1480 Window Rock, AZ 86515) or walk-in. If there is NO biological concerns, then a Biological Compliance Form will be issued. If concerns do arise, the client will need to select another Proposed Homesite in Area 3 or 4 from the RCP Map.

The third step was one I forgot about, and I couldn't complete it until two years later. This required us to go to Navajo Fish and Wildlife in Window Rock and provide a money order for $20, payable to the Navajo Nation. The form was completed on September 19, 2018. The Department of Fish

FIGURE 6.1 Photo shows Delores Greyeyes pointing out the stakes set out by
the land surveyor. This photo was taken August 1, 2021, by Wendy Greyeyes.

and Wildlife issued a "Homesite Biological Clearance Form."[4] The form
stated, "Biological review has determined the Homesite Lease will not
significantly impact the wildlife resources, threatened, and endangered
species including plants and their habitat." This was the final form required
for the completion of my HSL agreement.

    4. Archaeological Clearance:
        a. Client will need to hire a Private Archaeologist at their own ex-
           pense to conduct a cultural resource investigation on the Proposed
           Homesite and report the findings to Navajo Historic Preservation
           Department for review. Client is responsible for submitting a copy
           of their receipt to NLD once completed.

This step began on July 7, 2015, which required another money order to-
taling $200.00 plus the Navajo Nation sales tax of $10.00. We received
the Archaeological Inventory Report on March 21, 2016. In the report, it

described any prior projects that occurred in the area. It also described any traditional cultural properties (TCP) in the area. It stated there was nothing within 1 acre of the HSL. The report also stated the Area Environmental and Cultural Setting, which described the nearest major water source 157 feet to the northeast, and vegetation consisted of a juniper tree, pine trees, snakeweed, cholla cactus, Russian thistle, sage brush, and Indian rice grass. It also described the impact of a home building as heavy erosion and blading for road maintenance. The archaeological review did approve the continuation for a homesite lease.[5]

5. Navajo Nation Heritage and Historic Preservation Department (HPD):
    a. HPD shall issue a Cultural Resources Compliance Form (CRCF) if there are no archaeological concerns. Client is responsible for submitting a copy of the approved CRCF to NLD once complete.

The Historic Preservation Department's CRCF was also issued by the Project Archaeologist. They inspected the site on February 21, 2015, and issued the report on January 4, 2016. The report was completed with the signature and approval by the Bureau of Indian Affairs Navajo Regional Office on June 14, 2016. This report states the type of investigation of the site, and if any cultural resources, eligible properties, noneligible properties, and archaeological resources were found. The results showed none were found.[6]

6. Legal Survey
    a. Client will need to hire a Certified Land Surveyor at their own expense to conduct a civil survey and survey plat for the Proposed Homesite. Client is responsible for submitting a copy of their receipt and survey plat to NLD once complete.

The land surveyor was with Red Valley Survey from Shiprock, New Mexico, by Henry Thomas for the state of Arizona. We paid him $380.00 for his services. In this survey, he evaluated the area to figure out where the powerline was, the waterline, and to map out the precise location of the homesite lease. We came to discover that due to the land area, my homesite lease would only be .70 acres. The legal description states, "A parcel of land located in the Northwest quarter (NW1/4) of Section 5, Protracted Township 37 North, Range 18 East, G&SRM, Navajo County, Arizona, also situate in the Kayenta area and being more particularly described as follows." This was completed on September 29, 2015.[7]

7. Environmental Compliance Determination (ECD)
    a. General Land Department will conduct an Environmental Review of the Proposed Homesite. If there are NO Environmental concerns, a Clearance letter will be issued to the client. If a concern does arise a full-fledged Environmental Assessment will be required if the client still wishes to pursue that same location.

The Environmental Protection Agency offered their account and approval for my homesite on September 17, 2018. The form stated:

The Navajo Nation Environmental Protection Agency (NNEPA) recommends approval for the proposed +1.00 acres to Wendy Greyeyes. The proposed homesite lease action will not significantly impact the Navajo Nation's environmental resources. Any utility extensions right of way(s) outside the homesite lease will require a complete environmental assessment(s). Any new access road(s) will require cultural, biological, and environmental resources before blading and/or clearing the land surface. This environmental clearance is only for the 1.00 acres homesite lease. Utility extensions within the homesite lease are approved. The Bureau of Indian Affairs Real Estate may proceed with a Categorical Exclusion for the proposed homesite lease action. This was approved by the Navajo Nation's Executive Director.[8]

8. Navajo Land Department Director Approval
    a. Upon verification for quality assurance by the NLD Agency Offices, the Homesite Lease Application package will be submitted to the NLD Manager, Mike Halona who will review and give final approval on behalf of the Navajo Nation.
    b. If approved, copies of the approved Homesite Lease will be sent to the client, BIA, and Southwest Title Plant-Albuquerque, NM for recording.
    c. The first year's HSL Rental Fee is expected to be paid before receiving your approved Homesite Lease. In the amount of $12 through a money order, made payable to the Navajo Nation.

After we completed the forms, we submitted the forms to the Tuba City Land Department in January 2016 with a money order for $30.00. We didn't hear from the land department for nearly two years. Finally, I drove to Tuba City, Arizona, to find out what happened. I was directed to Saint Michaels, Arizona, to the main land department office. From there, I learned there was still a missing Fish and Wildlife document. Unfortunately, it took two years to finally hear from the department to help process my claim. It became very clear at that point the staff at the land department had not only misplaced files but contact information on the website was outdated. I voiced my concerns and shared copies of my homesite file. I wrote a long email on October 10, 2018, to the director of the land department articulating my concerns and the demands upon Navajos to return home, which I share here:

Dear Mike,

Hi. My name is Wendy Greyeyes and I have been working to get a homesite lease at Tsegi, AZ since 2014. I am writing to respectfully ask if I can write an email to the Tuba City land department supervisor to use an email to suffice as written permission for my mom to pick up my homesite application.

Today I received a call from Tanya at the Navajo Land Department informing me my documents needed a signature and check. Since I do not live near Tuba City, my mom offered to pick up the documents and bring to me for signature. I had a difficult time with the supervisor—who would not share her name and hung up on me. She informed me she had paperwork due today that needed to be in Window Rock. I explained my situation and the supervisor explained that I needed to have a written explanation that my mom would be picking up these documents on my behalf. I asked if I could email this to her. I felt the supervisor became unhelpful and lacked customer service skills to understand the situation to coordinate with my mom to pick up these documents. She would not permit me but instead said that she would have the documents sent to Kayenta Township. This was not what I was asking and the conversation became extremely tense.

As my mom and I have explained, our documents were submitted three years ago (signed, all the attachments, and a check). Since then, we have learned that a new staffing has been established at the Tuba City land office. We recognize that the Navajo Nation homesite process is slow—but I felt that your supervisor did not show me the respect and candor necessary to help work out a way to get me the documents for my signature. I also felt that with my specific experience, that the Tuba City land office had previously lost my documents—at least the supervisor would work with me. I also explained to her that I did make an attempt three weeks ago and came to the Window Rock Homesite Lease office to sign these same documents— unfortunately you were at a conference. I believe I have made a strong effort to follow the process step-by-step.

So in light of my due diligence to get my homesite lease processed, I am requesting that the Navajo Land Department accept a written email (with a hand written note and my signature attached) serve as my waiver to give my mom the authority to pick up my application. My mom will be coming to Albuquerque this weekend and I can sign the documents. She will be driving through Tuba City next week and can drop these documents off on my behalf. I am respectfully asking that you accommodate my request.

I know you may have heard this over and over—but I am pleading that your staff do their best to work with individuals trying to get their homesite lease. Many of us want to return home. But this type of treatment and lack of empathy is very frustrating. Although, I still have faith in our tribal process and its my hope you will honor my request.

Respectfully yours,

Dr. Wendy Greyeyes[9]

After this email, the director responded the next day and provided guidance on Friday, October 12, 2018, at 4:30 p.m.

Dr. Greyeyes,
Thanks for bring your concerns to my attention. Receiving feed back from our clients does help in improving our services to the Navajo people.

I remember your homesite application (copy) was brought directly to me at my office because it was missed place at the Tuba City Land Office. I was informed that you would come by and sign your lease. Apparently, that did not happen.

I'll have Ms. Lenora Tsosie, Senior Program Project Specialist contact you and figure out how to get your signature and money order so you will have a finalized approved homesite lease. Further delays in you obtaining your homesite lease should not occur.

Ms. Tsosie is cc'd in this email.

If you have any additional questions don't hesitate to contact me directly. Thanks.

Mike Halona

Navajo Land Department[10]

Afterward, the Senior Project Specialist reached out by email directly to my mom. It was an extremely passive-aggressive move to ignore my emails and go directly to my mom. She informed us by email the paperwork was ready for my signature to finalize the homesite lease. On October 18, 2018, I drove to Tuba City. The woman I was critical of in my email was at the office. I met with her and she was extremely pleasant and kind. She read through the entire agreement that required my signature.[11] The agreement shows an assigned lease number, and it states the lease is entered into by and between the Navajo Nation and the lessor. My census number is listed and cites the Navajo Nation code, "2 N.N.C. §§ 501 (B) (2) and (3), 16 N.N.C. § 2301, and Resolution No. RDCO-74–16 of the Resources Committee of the Navajo Nation Council, the provisions of 25 U.S.C. § 415 (e) as implemented by the regulations in 25 C.F.R. Part 162, the Navajo Nation General Leasing Act regulations, the Navajo Nation Homesite Policies and Procedures regulations, and all amendments or successors thereto, which by this reference are made a part thereof." The regulations and explanation of the entire document took at least an hour as she covered "Definitions," "Use of Leased Premises," "Term," "Rent," "Development of Leased Premises; Improvements," "Delivery of Premises; Customary Use Rights," "Inheritance," "Assignment," "Encumbrance," "Default," "Sanitation," "Hazardous Substances," "Termination of Federal Supervision," "Interest of Member of Congress," "Obligations to the Navajo Nation," "Eminent Domain," "Minerals," "Governing Law and Choice of Forum," "Consent to Jurisdiction; Covenant Not to Contest Jurisdiction," "No Waiver of Sovereign Immunity," "Successors and Assigns," "Superseding Lease Indenture," and "Notices." As we walked through the terms, impact of the lease expires on October 10, 2093. A seventy-five-year lease in which anything I build and invest in would be given back to the Navajo Nation.

I left the office and returned to my parents' home. We talked about this process. In total, we spent about $670.00 in fees, not including the gas and travel between Albuquerque, New Mexico, and the Navajo Nation. I work at the University of New Mexico, which is 322 miles (4 hours, 30 minutes) one-way, and the drive back and forth takes a tremendous toll. We started this work on August 4, 2014, and concluded it on October 18, 2018. This effort took four years and two months. Clearly, my parents played a pivotal role in helping shape the home-building process. I must consider $670 is a lot of money for any Navajo family. On the Navajo Nation, most families do not have an extra $670 to push through the paperwork and to make calls, or to go to these offices during their business office hours from Monday to Friday, 8:00 a.m. to 5:00 p.m. Most Navajos work during these times, and take time off to run these errands, including traveling to Window Rock, Arizona, several times to complete the forms.

The next steps for me are to pay the annual rent and begin building my home. Instead of getting a money order each year to pay the annual amount of $12.00 to the Navajo Nation land department, I paid for five years and sent a money order to the land department, making sure it clearly stated, "Navajo Nation." Otherwise, in my situation, my personal check was returned by postage and my money order had to be reissued because I did not clearly state "Navajo Nation" on the "To" line on the money order.

Building a home has its own ups and downs. I started to review the mortgage loan process. A lot of questions and concerns have cropped up as I've been completing the paperwork for the Navajo Partnership for Housing to qualify for a loan. I've had to work on my credit, which involved paying off a tremendously high student loan. In 2022 I began the process of home building; however, as many homeowners have cautioned, everything is tremendously expensive and one should wait until the market declines, which is especially important for home building. I've also had to reach out to NTUA to find out the cost of bringing water and electricity to my home. NTUA informed me that I needed to provide the homesite lease agreement, the archaeology survey report, the cultural document, project request form, compliance form, water forms, my social security card, and Certificate of Indian Blood.[12] All the documents would be given to the engineering department to begin the process for water and electricity. They also informed me I would need to pay for the expenses to have water and electricity brought to my homesite area. I reached out to a home builder, and she informed me that in her previous home-building experiences, the cost can be as high as $25,000. As I consider these additional hurdles, I also must consider maintaining my job in Albuquerque, New Mexico. With each additional move to build a home, this return to home seems so much farther away as I feel the high cost to have my own home on the Navajo Nation.

FORM NN200RL   **THE NAVAJO NATION**   LEASE NO.

April, 2017

HOMESITE LEASE
(Tribal Member Only)
(Trust or Restricted Land Only)

THIS LEASE is made and entered into by and between THE NAVAJO NATION, P.O. Box 9000, Window Rock, Navajo Nation (Arizona) 86515,

("Lessor"), and _____   _____, C#_____

and _____, C#_____

whose address is _____

("Lessee") in accordance with 2 N.N.C. §§ 501 (B) (2) and (3), 16 N.N.C. § 2301, and Resolution No. RDCO-74-16 of the Resources Committee of the Navajo Nation Council, the provisions of 25 U.S.C. § 415 (e) as implemented by the regulations contained in 25 C.F.R. Part 162, the Navajo Nation General Leasing Act regulations, the Navajo Nation Homesite Policies and Procedures regulations, and all amendments or successors thereto, which by this reference are made a part hereof. In the event this Lease is held by two or more persons, it shall be held in the following tenure:

N/A

WITNESSETH:

1.   DEFINITIONS.

      (A). "Approved Encumbrance" means an encumbrance approved in writing by the Lessor.

      (B). "Encumbrancer" means the owner and holder of an Approved Encumbrance, or either of them.

2.   LEASED PREMISES. For and in consideration of the rents, covenants, agreements, terms and conditions contained herein, Lessor hereby leases to Lessee all that tract or parcel of land situated within the _____Kayenta_____ Chapter of the Navajo Nation, (County of ____Navajo____, State of _____Arizona_____) which is more particularly described in Exhibit "A" attached hereto and by this reference made a part hereof, containing approximately _0.70_ acre(s), more or less, subject to any prior, valid existing rights-of-way. There is hereby reserved and accepted from the leased premises rights-of-way for utilities constructed by or on authority of Lessor.

3.   USE OF LEASED PREMISES.

      (A). Lessee shall develop, use, and occupy the leased premises for residential purposes only and said premises shall not be used for any other purpose. Lessee may construct, improve, and maintain a dwelling and related structures on the leased premises and may otherwise develop, use, or occupy said premises for residential purposes only.

      (B). Lessee agrees not to use or cause to be used any part of the leased premises for any unlawful conduct or purpose.

4.   TERM. Lessee shall have and hold the leased premises for a term of beginning on _October 10, 2018_ and ending on _October 9, 2093_. This Lease may be renewed for an additional primary term by approval of the Navajo Land Department, provided that this Lease is in good standing at the time of application. Lessee shall give written notice of intent to renew this Lease to the Department Manager of the Navajo Land Department, or its successor agency or department, at least six (6) months, but no more than twelve (12) months, prior to the expiration date of this Lease. Renewal of

FIGURE 6.2 Navajo Nation homesite lease agreement. This agreement removes identifiers related to the author but shows the first page of a seven-page agreement.

As I analyze my experience, I must factor in some other thoughts about the bigger picture. I recognize home ownership through land leasing does not coincide with the nature of a person's lifetime employment. During a person's lifetime, a person may have up to seven different jobs requiring the person to move from one community to the next to seek these job opportunities. In my personal experience, I've moved quite frequently for my own career path, from Kayenta, Arizona (two jobs); Phoenix, Arizona (four jobs); Window Rock, Arizona (three jobs); Washington, DC (one job); and now to Albuquerque, New Mexico (one job). In my lifetime so far, I've had eleven jobs requiring me to move. It is extremely rare to meet an older person who has maintained one job for their entire career, leading to retirement. But even these long-term jobs lead to anguish and burnout for those employed, creating a class of exhausted workers continuing to work within the Navajo Nation. With these hurdles, the effort by Navajos to favor home purchasing off Navajo land and to manage homesites is not an uncommon response by our people.

As we see these numbers shift, we must acknowledge there is a lack of affordable homes for Navajos working on the reservation, which is a significant challenge for the generation of Navajos seeking jobs. Many times, the employer is responsible for providing housing during the person's work tenure. Homesite lease approvals can take from 9 months to 24 months, according to the Homesite Land Department.[13] In many cases, this is not the situation. The process can be as long as two to five years, due to the bureaucratic processing of acquiring signatures from neighbors a half mile within your desired land lease area, archeological and biological clearances, land surveyed, and the land department's process.

With this stated, Navajos are migratory. This observation of Navajos is not new. This echoes back to our sheep camp movements when we moved from our winter to summer camps to protect livestock. We have always moved to follow our core economic survival—our sheep. Many data points capture one point in time, typically capturing one primary locale for which people are economically dependent. So, data points that tell the story we are a stagnant group locked into one place must be treated with suspicion. A scholar of Navajo people must find data points that capture the essence of migratory movements. Myla Vicenti Carpio, an American Indian Studies professor at Arizona State University, in *Indigenous Albuquerque*, shows that Pueblos, Jicarilla Apaches, and Navajos are constantly returning to their homelands for social, cultural, and familial obligations. This is evident in the third wave of urban Indigenous movements.[14] In the first wave of urban Indian migration, the distances between city and reservation (physical and cultural) were further and traveling home was rare or impossible. In the second wave, the city and reservation became closer as car ownership and freeways made it more accessible. In the third wave, technology has strengthened the cultural linkage.[15] Carpio's research shows Navajo people are making continuous moves to engage and stay connected to our Navajo communities.

In this next part of my chapter, I will describe the history of movement on our land through literature reviews synthesizing our understandings and relationship to the land. Second, I will describe the demographic shifts of our people, contributions of movers on/off Navajo lands, and finally, reframing consciousnesses of "rez versus urban" language to attitudes of migratory Navajos. The importance of understanding our complex history is imperative to know the source of the lateral animosity stated in the epigraph. It is my hope with this chapter that we remember how our Navajo Nation got to this point and acknowledge that our relationship to the land has deep colonial roots prompting these lateral animosities. We must change the language of how we comprehend the connection to our homelands and not weaponize land ownership as a divisive tool upon our own people.

We Move for Our Survival

Navajo people are built to move, change, and create. In our creation stories, our ancestors migrated through the four worlds to escape the monsters that would destroy our existence.[16] After moving out of four worlds and into our current world, our ancestors constructed this world that is embraced by the land itself. The Holy People established the mountains and the sacred places that would define our new home. But the meaning of these established spaces of home did not mean a self-quarantined zone that kept us in an imprisoned space. Instead, home was identified by markers as a recognition of our entrance into the world. These markers are our anchor to the rest of the world. As Navajos, we recognized land as a porous and borderless reality. We were not built to stand in one place. We move for our survival by building relationships with others and crossing terrains to conduct trade, work, politick, and learn. This has been always the case—just as Changing Woman created the first people with the original clans. As of today, we have more than one hundred clans that reflect our movement and engagement with others. We connect and build relationships for our survival that go beyond the four original clans. Our survival is based on a history of migration. We move to exist. It is important to recognize the foundational elements of our existence that help us unpackage the literature and perceptions of land.

It is important to see how in the literature about Navajo land, many meanings exist that have been examined through differing lenses, from Navajo to Anglo-American worldviews. It is extremely critical to understand how land is perceived by Navajo people and Euro-Anglo people who rely heavily upon the precolonial to postcolonial, and to honor Vine Deloria's own term, *recolonization*, as part of the postcolonial. These periods carry with them the cultural and dominating moods that have shaped our relationship to the land that has stemmed from its destruction to its growth, beginning with "Precontact" with Euro-Anglos' "Colonization" and "Postcolonial/Decolonization/Recolonization." The literature around land is important to help contextualize Navajo worldviews of land.

Precolonial Purity

I examine the precolonial period from the perspectives of Navajo and Anglo to give a synopsis of both literature and personal perceptions of land to situate our precolonial conceptions of land dictating our reality. In other words, land served as a reference point and the environment shaped the planting seasons. The environment shaped our bodies through migration from winter to summer camps, day/night transformations, and planting seasons, and the eclipse creates a reset for our bodies. The land impacts our bodies, especially when we use land as a reference point. It stems from our need to rest at night and awake when the sun rises. Women's menstrual cycles are aligned to the monthly full moons.

Our social relationships are also built around the land as a mother. For Navajo, the land was owned by the matriarch. During marriage, the man would move to the family's home. The land referenced and anchored the matriarchal power within the relations. Land contains our sacred mountains and spaces that were provided by the Holy People. Private property was not for an individual but was held by families and extended clans. To contrast this, the Anglo view of Navajo land is that it was unoccupied and uncivilized. The language of terra nullius implies nothing exists in the land and it is open for taking, which was conceptualized about our lands and territories.

Precontact describes the period described by the Diné as our state of purity, prior to contact. These are in our original stories in which *precolonial* means that Indigenous people were able to continue to live in a state of balance and harmony with their own values to protect the land. American Indians hold their lands as *places*—as having the highest possible meaning—and all their statements are made with this reference in point. In contrast, Western societies derive meaning from the world in historical and developmental terms, thereby placing *time* as the narrative as central importance.[17] In our creation stories, our ancestors migrated through the four worlds to escape the monsters that would destroy our existence.[18] In each world, Navajos perfected their local knowledge in order to defy efforts to destroy the people. Our precolonial realities valued the stories of our migration and how to survive upon the distinctive terrain of our lands. In contrast, the Western view is that the Indigenous land was terra nullius, unoccupied.[19] This basic belief led to the justification of the next period of transformation for Indigenous people in the United States, when we entered the colonial period.

Colonial Contamination

Colonial agents took the terra nullius conception and began the destruction of Indigenous lands by contaminating the waters, soil, and sky in the name of building a new republic. This new republic espoused values of property, freedom, and equality for all. Unfortunately, Indigenous peoples were not afforded these same entitlements. Instead, the new republic took over and killed Indigenous peoples for impeding the Western goal of civilization. No longer is land viewed as a reference point for our human reality; instead the institutionalization of a time-controlled human reality began to embed itself into the foundation of our minds and applied to our lands.

In the work of Nicholas C. Zaferatos, he describes these oppositional forces of the political economy under three elements:

1. Self-Governance and Sovereignty—Government policy diminishing
    tribal self-governance; state and local powers which created private
    opposition to tribal governance.
2. Territoriality and Natural Resources—Assimilation and incorporation
    of reservation resources which created non-Indian reservation occu-
    pancy and ownership of reservation assets.
3. Tribal Sufficiency and Social Cohesiveness—Social fragmentation,
    cultural assimilation, and alienation which created restricted access to
    capital and reservation economic alienation.[20]

Zaferatos shows how these oppositional forces within the period of colonialism has constructed the current state of our access to our own lands,
resources, and social cohesion. The importance of understanding these
oppositional forces is to see there is a tremendous disconnect triggered by
settler colonialists that bleed our lands for their own wealth and left Native
peoples without access to their resources. This contextualizes the highly
bureaucratic system of the Navajo Nation's Homesite Lease process. This
is especially evident in the language of the Navajo Nation's Homesite Lease
Agreement. We do not own the land we build our homes upon. The challenge is that the Navajo Nation does not fully own their lands because
of the complex process of leasing where individualized land holdings is
not permitted. Recently, 2022 Navajo Nation presidential candidate Ethel
Branch discussed how this process worked, its added challenges to addressing intergenerational poverty, and the process to reverse our continuous effort to address these issues.[21] She articulated that by allowing
individuals to own the property, they could sell portions of their property
to buy the much-needed infrastructure, like solar panels, wells, electricity,
and other needs to help ignite an economic lift that invests in the land and
their homes.

    In my previous work as an intern with Diné Policy Institute, we dis-
cussed these issues of land reform in many community discussions. From
these discussions, it is very clear that Navajos do not want anyone near
their homesite or grazing lands, and to bring the issue to the forefront
required a need to educate on the history of land ownership. This includes
Navajo Nation leaders' own anticipation of giving the lands to the families because we do not have faith in our own people. This fear is driven
by dependency. Robert J. Miller describes the meanings and impacts of
dependency. He writes, "Tribal communities that had fed, clothed, and

supported themselves for thousands of years gradually began to rely on non-Indians for manufactured goods, clothing, and food."[22] We have also relied on non-Indians for our education, constructing a consciousness of our own self-conceptions of resilience and autonomy, which is that we do not have this self-sovereign awareness. Our educational institutions have robbed our children of independent critical consciousness and self-awareness.[23] I also believe during this time, we should acknowledge movements have occurred within our Navajo communities.

In the literature around land and migration, "pull and push" factors are driven by economic and social necessity. Migration authors describe this period as "Migrations in an Age of Globalization."[24] The age of globalization kicked off with approximately 170 million men and women leaving their homes to fight in one of the world wars, including our Navajo men.[25] We are part of this globalized world event, evident after many Navajo men returned home and filled political positions in the Navajo Tribal Council. Their exposure to cities, peoples, and different cultures reconstituted their awareness and consciousness of where Navajos fall in this global network.

Many Navajos have placed their children and spouses at the center of their decision-making. Others have placed their education as the core. And many have made it a point to push for a career fulfilling their dreams of being the top in their field. These motivations drive decisions by Navajos to leave our homeland for jobs, stable salaries, healthy working spaces, affordable homes, amenities, and educational experiences. It is not easy to leave Nihikéyah with the beauty of the sunsets and changing seasons. It is not easy to leave the familiar faces of our family and friends. The shock of border towns and urban enclaves of whites, blacks, Asians, Hispanics, and others creates new norms and realities for Navajo people during this period of colonization. As we consider the notions of a new period, or the possibility of self-determination shaping this conception of self-governance and self-determination, the next section turns to postcolonial prayers.

This period led to the theft of millions of acres of land through treaties, forced migration, and colonial military violence. This is very well documented in the works of Vine Deloria Jr. and Clifford Lytle's *The Nation Within: The Past and Future of American Indian Sovereignty*.[26] Deloria and Lytle describe the congressional moves to establish Indian reservations as a strategy to strengthen the federal government's oversight and control of Indian tribes. They describe how the reservation system was established by Indian agents with some tribes adopting it easily. But many others resisted. This was easily the case for the Navajo people, as many viewed the federal government with massive disdain and distrust. As we see, the Navajo people articulated the need to educate the children, but as we have learned, the boarding school experience was also a ruse to further control Indian lands and to teach children to have disdain toward their community and their people. Colonialism is the practice by which a powerful country directly controls less powerful countries and uses its resources to increase its own power and wealth.[27] The effort by the federal government to move Native Americans from a state of savagery to a civilized state encoded into the Navajo population a sense of a time-controlled human reality.[28] Through the coupling of forced education and language learning, Indigenous children were being taught the meaning of private property, individualism, and wage ownership described by David Adams.[29] It's also clear that the false government constructed by the federal government in the 1920s describes the period of exploitation of the Navajo people's lands.[30] Land is viewed here as an object that contains valuable minerals and resources. The perception of land as a living being is pushed to the back side as early leaders signed off on gas, coal, and oil leases that lead to the extractive economy that helped shape and define our current state of land issues—although the extractive economic system supported many families, as it offered jobs for Navajo families. I recognize that I benefited from my father's forty years working for both Peabody Coal Mine and Kayenta Coal Mine, but it has left devastating effects. With the shutdown of the mines, many mine workers are forced to move off the reservation for jobs. Some workers have become sick, especially with the remnants of uranium mines that have left Navajo families caring for their elders and paying for much needed treatment. It's unclear how much of this extractive economy has impacted the animals, the forestry, and water. This has brought many activists to the forefront to push back against our own leadership with homegrown organizations like the Black Mesa Water Coalition, Tó Nizhóní Ání (Sacred Water Speaks). These organizations have forced our people to think about what the future holds for our people and how we must consider sustainable economies that need to help our people and our mother earth to heal. We have given too much of our power to the federal government and outsiders. It's time to consider the new movements happening internally and externally.

Postcolonial Prayers

Many scholars have debated the meaning and significance of our existence in a postcolonial period. Elizabeth Cook-Lynn argues we have never exited out of colonialism.[31] Kevin Bruyneel's work points out that 1871 was the turn toward postcolonial time in U.S. Indigenous relations. 1871 is the year of the end of treaty-making, which is the basis of his interpretation of postcolonial.[32] Leela Gandhi, writing about India, provides a different way to consider postcolonial thinking. She writes, "This period of colonization has radically moved us out of a purity of our own pre-colonial relationships to the land and to each other. Postcolonial is a theoretical resistance to the mystifying amnesia of the colonial aftermath devoted to the task of revisiting, remembering, and crucially, interrogating the colonial past; more sensitive to the long history of colonial consequences."[33] Although the United States of America, a colonial power, has not exited our Indigenous homelands, we are in a state of retooling our governing systems. This begins with interrogating the impacts of the colonial past, including artifacts like the Homesite Lease and Navajo Nation Codes that have hindered our ability to be a true sovereign nation. These artifacts create an imposed colonial order of our lands and our laws. I describe these as artifacts because they are imitating colonial constructs of legitimacy. As we decolonize our systems of power, we have to examine these artifacts and their impact. As Andrew Curley terms fate as the "story of Navajo legibility,"[34] which is the process of standardization and simplification, so we become easily conquerable. This unification of our realities into flat sheets of paper allow for our realities to be truncated into data points forcing us to be controlled and managed. In a postcolonial reimagining, we must break from this oversimplification and standardization and return to our postcolonial conceptions of precolonial hopes and dreams. We must also make room in the land discourse recognizing movement and growth. I highlight our demographic transformation that must be factored into our discussion around postcolonial prayers.

- Navajo Nation is transforming demographically reporting that 172,813[35] currently reside on the Navajo Nation, with a reported 399,999 that are enrolled with the Navajo Nation.[36] In 2022, during the Kiva Club Powwow at the University of New Mexico, Navajo Nation President

Jonathan Nez announced that the Navajo enrollment surpassed the 400,000 number. With these numbers, it is clear more than half of the Navajo Nation population lives off our homeland.

- The future population relies on women to give birth to children. The data show there are more females at 51.9 percent of the population; the remainder 48.1 percent are men. This creates challenges for Navajo women to find a mate to copulate and repopulate the next generation of Navajos. But this comes with the added challenge that future babies will not be born into marriage families, as marriage-coupled families are only at 34.3 percent on the Navajo Nation. The female householder with no spouse present and with family is at 26.8 percent. Those that have never been married is at 53.3 percent.[37]

- The largest employer on the Navajo Nation is the government that provides education, health care, and social services for its peoples. The Navajo government receives 75 percent of their funding from federal transfers to cover salaries, education, health care, tribal colleges, social services, public safety, and transportation. When a person finds a job, housing becomes more problematic because it is often unavailable. Instead, 17.2 percent of workers ($n = 49,014$) find themselves commuting over an hour out.[38] The Navajo Nation is described as being as large as the state of West Virginia.

Postcolonial means occurring or existing after the end of colonial rule. But this is a highly debatable discussion because some argue that colonialism has not ended, but instead we have constructed a "cyborg of postcoloniality [that] is also plagued by 'something like an imperative to grow new organs, to expand or sensorium and our body to some new, yet unimaginable, perhaps impossible, dimensions.'"[39] The conception of a postcolonial reality must involve the people. As Ezra Rosser reminds the Navajo People, they are the ones with the decision-making power to exert their sovereignty.[40] To make this move, we observed how the presidential candidates articulated these issues around dated terminology of "economic development" and "bringing our Navajo youth home to help build a new Navajo." Many of us have heard these slogans, and this has not inspired transformation in our communities or incited change. We need new terminology that helps us consider the future of our Indigenous reality. Vine Deloria Jr. coined the term "recolonization," which he describes as natives gradually returning to and reclaiming their rightful places in their former homelands. This would be about nations united to retake lands, power, and ideas.[41]

This movement will require the Navajo people to call out the United States for its participation in the taking and exploitative nature of these lands. The recolonization movement involves examining these moral questions, which may be included in the current discussions around the Landback movement. The Landback movement raises an old and unanswered moral question for the United States and for our tribal nations. The Landback rhetoric forces our society to consider how to fix the injustices of America's colonial past. Future research must examine how the Landback rhetoric brings to the surface our moral obligation as a democratic nation to repair the wrongs of our colonial past—especially with recent Land Acknowledgement statements being read by government, universities, and corporations that recognize where these institutions are built. If Landback becomes a reality, the demands by activists and leaders is the return of the jurisdictional and sovereign oversight of lands. This type of action will force the federal government to revisit the approximately 368 treaties that were negotiated and signed by U.S. commissioners and tribal leaders from 1777 to 1868 to determine territories that must be returned. But, on the other hand, a historic move like this will also force tribal leaders to retool and rethink their tribal institutions' jurisdictional oversight.

The Landback movement articulated by current Native American activists is a call for the return of stolen Native American lands and territories in the United States. Landback rhetoric has heightened due to social movements such as the No Dakota Access Pipeline (NoDAPL), the movement to protect Bear's Ears, and preventing fracking at Chaco Canyon. These social movements are in response to the United States' destructive stewardship of lands with destabilizing impacts upon sacred lands and spaces. The Landback rhetoric from Native American activists must be understood especially amid Native American leaders' governing goals. Native American leaders are elected to manage the affairs of their Native people. The activist's language is dismissed as too lofty or without intellectual grounding. But, intellectually, the Landback rhetoric is echoed in the language of leaders such as tribal sovereignty and the federal Indian trust relationship. Tribal sovereignty is understood by the United States as upholding federal trust relationships that were established through federal Indian treaties. The treaty period in the United States ended, but these agreements have been codified into U.S. statutes that guide and shape how the federal government engages with tribal nations. The missing part of the Landback movement is to understand the moral obligation embedded in the federal Indian trust relationship, which is a critical question for our American future. America recognizes that the genocide and theft of Native lands is immoral, but why has it not prompted the return of these lands to rectify the unspeakable acts imposed by colonization? If lands are not returned, what are the justifiable acts of restitution to compensate for these actions? What is the moral move for our country and the future of Indigenous relations in this period of federal trust responsibilities?

Entering the space of postcolonial prayers, we have to reshape our talk or we may lose another generation who will not return home to be the true leaders of our Navajo Nation. We cannot continue to challenge and undermine the choices of our Navajo people. Navajo people are working to strengthen our Navajo communities by balancing returning to the homeland and building community within urban spaces. Some remarks and comments made by families and friends living on the Navajo Nation generally imply there is a type of purity test at play. We have to reform this type of talk into ways of inviting and understanding the choices our Navajo people have made to leave home. We also need to think about how to create land reform that understands the emotional and traumatic connections of our people. Although there is a great number of non-Navajo lawyers and academics who write on issues of land reform, this must be driven by the Navajo people. We also must not place this change into Window Rock or a local community framework. There is tension between local communities. Some local communities are perceived as "cities" and others as "rural" communities. As I've listened to the 2022 presidential discussions and observed movements made in past administrations, we need a land reform policy based upon our own values as Diné.

Navajo Values / Navajo Land Reform Process

1. Patience—Listening and visiting all the communities on the Navajo Nation to capture the major issues of land and what it would mean to privatize homesite and grazing site leases.

2. Knowledge—Deep understanding of the history of the homesite lease process, home building process, entities like Navajo Tribal Utility Authority; probate and property laws; using clear language to help families understand; providing examples.

3. Relationship—Keeping connections to the community members and learning names, relationship to each other (clanship), continually revising and following up with the relations in the community.

4. Reciprocity—Returning to the communities and keeping the conversation focused on land reform. Determining those that would want to pursue this process of land reform.

5. Character—Ensuring the land reform team spends less time talking and more time listening; being honest, have a strong work ethic; show modesty, flexibility, Navajo cultural norms, teamwork.

6. Ethical methodology—Properly documenting visits, conversations, transcripts, sign-in sheets, recordings, and protecting information. Making sure that communities understand you are documenting and understanding when "No" means "No." Do not pressure or intimidate community members.

7. Timeliness and Metrics—Leadership administration is four years long. Recognizing that your timeline must include one year of community visits, reporting back to the community, developing a framework that is written and orally described will take time, and providing a plan. Recognize your own limitations and focus on the number of homesite leases and a goal for transforming those leases into ownership.

8. Research—Make sure to read and develop a listing of literature that discusses the possibilities of land reform. This can include books like *Creating Private Sector Economies in Native America: Sustainable Development Through Entrepreneurship* (2019) by editors Robert Miller, Miriam Jorgensen, and Daniel Stewart. Be real about using these resources, and recognize Navajo people are cautious of non-Navajos writing about Navajo people.

As I think through this colonial project, our Native American future depends on the consequences of our inaction (or action). There is a need to deepen our understanding of the Landback meanings and its relevance for the future. In my own work, I examined the Navajo Nation educational system with their effort to push their sovereign rights as a nation. Tribal nations are creatively developing strategies to create power from spaces of powerlessness. But the work examines the tribal nation working within the boundaries of the federal government. We should be asking the larger question of how we remove these boundaries and think bigger for our future as the Navajo people. Land is central to our understanding and relationship to Diné Bikéyah. The Landback movement creates the possibility of deploying a system that would give tribal nations full autonomy and claims over the jurisdiction of their own lands, institutions, and students. I am concerned with the possibilities of Landback as a postcolonial remedy as part of our moral commitment as a democratic nation.

Landback rhetoric raises the moral question for Americans. Its clear that moral questions of the U.S. colonial impact of theft and genocide of Native Americans has never received the national apology needed to begin healing. Instead, the U.S. government has constructed ideas of federal trust responsibilities, treaty obligations, and Indian land claims as ways to address the historical past. So, theories of reparations and reconciliation are ways in which the immoral acts of the past may find resolution for our future. Reparations is the act of making amends by paying through money or resources. Reconciliation is the act of finding common grounds with each other. Even after years of incorporating our Native American histories and experience into our educational systems, this has not led to the return of lands. Instead, Native America is seeing our nation split apart as an anti-truth movement, embraced by certain state legislatures that have prompted the call for "anti-woke" policies, which is a violation of our intellectual relationship with the truth of American history.

In an earlier article, I explored the work of Ezra Rosser's new book, *A Nation Within: Navajo Land and Economic Development*. I believe Rosser's work is an important book for conversations about Navajo economy and land development issues. Rosser states: "It is up to the Diné to decide for themselves" (160). This statement is accurate. As a Navajo woman, I've learned that if the people do not have a say in the solution, then there will be no buy-in. The Diné people have to seek out our own answers. I believe Ezra's work paints a powerful analysis of the condition of Navajo people and their relationship to the land. I think it was wise that Ezra Rosser did not write the recipe for how we can fix our reality but instead shined a light on where the tensions lie. We can work toward improving our fate to fulfill the dreams of a true sovereign nation. Ezra offers an important analysis of our history as the Navajo people, but it is clear that the fight remains with us.

Overall there must be a new vision under the postcolonial future. These Navajo values are based on policy processes I've encountered in my own community. They are based on my own mistakes and successes. But we must recognize our words, and language begins the movement toward social change and a future for our people that stems outmigration and poverty.

Notes

1. Navajo Nation Land Department Homesite Lease website, Navajo Nation Government, accessed February 18, 2022, http://nnld.org/home/homesite.
2. Jonathan D. Nez, "Field Clearance Certification for Homesite Lease Application," Navajo Nation Homesite Lease Application, Grazing Official/Land/Farm Board, October 15, 2014.
3. Jarrod Yazzie, "Homesite Lease Application (HSL) Checklist," Navajo Land Office, Tuba City, Arizona, November 2014.
4. Gloria M. Tom, "Homesite Biological Clearance Form," Navajo Nation Department of Fish and Wildlife, Window Rock, Arizona, October 23, 2015.
5. Santana B. Yazzie and Linda Laughing, "Archaeological Inventory Report Documentation Page," Navajo Nation Archaeology Department, Window Rock, Arizona, March 21, 2016.
6. Tamara Billie, "Cultural Resource Compliance Form," Navajo Nation Historic Preservation Department, Window Rock, Arizona, June 14, 2016.
7. Henry Thomas, "Homesite Lease Survey," Red Valley Survey, Shiprock, New Mexico, September 29, 2015.
8. Rita Whitehorse-Larsen, "Memorandum: Homesite Lease Wendy Shelly Greyeyes," Environmental Protection Agency, Window Rock, Arizona, March 4, 2016.
9. Wendy Greyeyes, "Homesite Lease Application—Wendy Greyeyes," email, October 11, 2018.
10. Mike Halona, "Re: Homesite Lease Application—Wendy Greyeyes," email, October 12, 2018.
11. Mike Halona, "Form NN200RL Homesite Lease: Tribal Member Only/Trust or Restricted Land Only," Navajo Nation Land Department, Window Rock, Arizona, October 10, 2018.
12. Personal Conversation with Marcella Black, Navajo Tribal Utility Authority, Kayenta, Arizona, October 1, 2020.
13. Navajo Nation Land Department Homesite Lease website, Navajo Nation Government, accessed February 18, 2022, http://nnld.org/home/homesite.
14. Myla Vicenti Carpio, *Indigenous Albuquerque* (Lubbock: Texas Tech University Press, 2011), 11.

15. Carpio, *Indigenous Albuquerque*, 6.

16. Klara Kelley and Harris Francis, *A Diné History of Navajoland* (Tucson: University of Arizona Press, 2019), 12.

17. Glen Coulthard, "From Wards of the State to Subjects of Recognition? Marx, Indigenous Peoples, and the Politics of Dispossession in Denendeh," in *Theorizing Native Studies*, eds. Audra Simpson and Andrea Smith (Durham and London: Duke University Press, 2014), 69.

18. Klara Kelley and Harris Francis, *A Diné History of Navajoland* (Tucson: University of Arizona Press, 2019), 12.

19. Ezra Rosser, *A Nation Within: Navajo Land and Economic Development* (New York: University of Cambridge Press, 2021), 9.

20. Nicholas C. Zaferatos, *Planning the American Indian Reservation: From Theory to Empowerment* (New York: Syracuse University Pres, 2015), 124.

21. Ethel Branch, meet and greet, May 22, 2022, Gloria Grant Home, Rio Rancho, N.M.

22. Robert J. Miller, *Reservation Capitalism: Economic Development in Indian Country* (Lincoln: University of Nebraska Press, 2012), 28.

23. Teresa L. McCarty, *A Place to Be Navajo: Rough Rock and the Struggle for Self-Determination in Indigenous Schooling* (Mahway, N.J.: Lawrence Erlbaum Associates, 2002); Sandy Grande, *Red Pedagogy: Native American Social and Political Thought* (Lanham: Rowman & Littlefield, 2015); Malia Villegas and Sabina Rak Neugebauer, eds., *Indigenous Knowledge and Education: Sites of Struggle, Strength and Survivance* (Cambridge: Harvard Education Publishing Group, 2008); Mary Battiste, *Decolonizing Education: Nourishing the Learning Spirit* (Saskatoon, SK, Canada: Purich Publishing, 2013).

24. Michael H. Fisher, *Migration: A World History* (New York: Oxford University Press, 2014), 104.

25. Fisher, *Migration*, 105.

26. Vine Deloria Jr. and Clifford M. Lytle, *The Nations Within: The Past and Future of American Indian Sovereignty* (Austin: University of Texas Press, 1984), 28–36.

27. Leela Gandhi, *Postcolonial Theory: A Critical Introduction*, 2nd ed. (New York: Columbia University Press, 2019), 4.

28. Coulthard "From Wards of the State to Subjects of Recognition?," 69.

29. David Wallace Adams, *Education for Extinction: American Indians and the Boarding School Experience* (1875–1928, 1995), chapter 1.

30. Robert Young, *A Political History of the Navajo Tribe.* (Tsaile: Navajo Community College Press, 1978), 49–52.

31. Jodi Byrd, "Still Waiting for the 'Post' to Arrive: Elizabeth Cook-Lynn and the Imponderables of American Indian Post-Coloniality," *Wicazo Sa Review* 31, no. 1 (2016): 75–89. https://experts.illinois.edu/en/publications/still-waiting-for-the-post-to-arrive-elizabeth-cook-lynn-and-the-.

32. Kevin Bruyneel, *The Third Space of Sovereignty: The Postcolonial Politics of U.S.-Indigenous Relations* (Minneapolis: University of Minnesota Press), 65.

33. Gandhi, *Postcolonial Theory*, 4.

34. Andrew Curley, "The Origin of Legibility: Rethinking Colonialism and Resistance Among the Navajo People, 1868–1937," *Diné Perspectives: Revitalizing and Reclaiming Navajo Thought*, ed. Lloyd L. Lee (Tucson: University of Arizona Press, 2014), 129.

35. U.S. Census Bureau, "Navajo Nation Reservation and Off-Reservation Land, AZ–NM–UT, Population 60 Years and Over in the United States," 2019 American Community Survey 5-Year Estimates, accessed January 15, 2022, https://data .census.gov/cedsci/table?t=Age%20and%20Sex%3AOlder%20Population%3A Populations%20and%20People&g=2500000US2430&tid=ACSST5Y2019.S0102.

36. Simon Romero, "Navajo Nation Becomes Largest Tribe in U.S. After Pandemic Enrollment Surge," *New York Times*, May 21, 2021, accessed February 18, 2022, https://www.nytimes.com/2021/05/21/us/navajo-cherokee-population.html.

37. U.S. Census Bureau, "Navajo Nation Reservation and Off-Reservation Land, AZ–NM–UT, Population 60 Years and Over in the United States," 2019 American Community Survey 5-Year Estimates, accessed January 15, 2022, https://data .census.gov/cedsci/table?t=Age%20and%20Sex%3AOlder%20Population%3A Populations%20and%20People&g=2500000US2430&tid=ACSST5Y2019.S0102.

38. U.S. Census Bureau, "Navajo Nation Reservation and Off-Reservation Land, AZ–NM–UT, Population 60 Years and Over in the United States," 2019 American Community Survey 5-Year Estimates, accessed January 15, 2022, https://data .census.gov/cedsci/table?t=Age%20and%20Sex%3AOlder%20Population%3A Populations%20and%20People&g=2500000US2430&tid=ACSST5Y2019.S0102.

39. Gandhi, *Postcolonial Theory*, 4.

40. Rosser, *A Nation Within*, 215.

41. David Wilkins, *Red Prophet: The Punishing Intellectualism of Vine Deloria, Jr* (Golden, CO: Fulcrum Publishing, 2018), 94–95.

NÁHOOKQS / NORTH

Winter on Nihikéyah. Courtesy of Lloyd L. Lee.

CHAPTER 7

The Footprints We Leave

Claiming Stewardship over Diné Bikéyah

REX LEE JIM

"Tell him that is Sis Naajiní," whispered into his ear the Child of the Wind.

"Tell him that is *Tsoodził*, the turquoise mountain," whispered the Child of the Wind.

"Tell him that is Dook'o'oosłííd, the abalone mountain, the holy mountain," whispered the Child of the Wind.

"Tell him that is Dibé Nitsaa, the jet mountain, the holy mountain, the chief mountain," whispered the Child of the Wind.

"Tell him that is Dził Ná'oodiłii, the soft goods mountain, the holy mountain, the chief mountain, everlasting mountain," whispered the Child of the Wind.

"Tell him that is Dził Ch'óol'į'į, the spruce mountain, the hard goods mountain, the holy mountain, the chief mountain, everlasting mountain, the mountain of beauty," whispered the Child of the Wind.

And pointing to Dził Ná'oodiłii, Naayéé' Neizghání, Monster Slayer, and Tó Bájíshchíní, Child Born of Water, proclaimed, "That is where we started from. That is where our mother White Shell Woman lives. That is where our mother Changing Woman lives. This is our home." With breath, with words and language, with wisdom, the twin warriors claimed stewardship over Diné Bikéyah.

Naayéé' Neizghání and Tó Bájíshchíní stood by their father Jóhonaa'áí, Day Carrier, in full regalia, centered and balanced. They just passed the final test by their father. The twin warriors claimed with their breath *Diné Bikéyah*, through their knowledge of the land, and naming each mountain meaningfully. They breathed in the land and became one with the land between the sacred mountains, exerting sovereignty over the land forever, the land beneath their feet, *bikee' biyaagi—akék'eh hashchíín*—committing to care for all places we step. Child of the Wind, or to be closer to the Navajo wording, Child of the Air, which is us with the "breath" standing within, coming and going, breathing in and out, that life force which sustains us, constantly reminding us of what we already know. This story shows that through our breath, our inner voices, our words we claim stewardship over the land. The dramatic exchange between the Warrior Twins and their father Day Carrier proclaims sovereignty over Navajo country, the kind that does not claim dominion over the land and every creature living on it. It is the kind of claim that is immediately relational, respectful, reciprocal, and reverent—*k'é bee t'áálá'í dzizlį́į́'*. We became one with all creation. We will care for the land for all living relations.

During a Blessing Way ceremony, at the end of a prayer, as patients we are asked to press the mountain bundle, a bundle of dirt taken from all the sacred mountains, thus our land, to our chest four times, then to breath in the mountain bundle four times, and finally to press the sacred bundle against our bodies from our feet to our head, becoming one with the mountains, with the land. Breathing in the mountains is one of the major keys to Navajo notion of inherent sovereignty—breathing in. Bił ani<u>dziih</u> is the phrase in Navajo: bił ani<u>dz</u>iih, ni<u>dz</u>iil, naniłdzil, **dzi**ł, hółdzil (breathe it in, you're strong, exercise, mountain, strong foundation—quick rough translations). The root of all these words is **dzi—breathing/strength**. Ultimately, the key to sustained sovereignty is the ability to breathe—to breathe in the necessary teachings so our children, our land, our government, our songs and prayers will keep us breathing and strong. Breathing is what keeps us moving forward, taking one step at a time.

Beginning the Walk with Songs

Naming is important. In Navajo, place names offer an entire way of life, of a mind-set that makes a people strong. We have the names of the sacred mountains. All things begin in the east and start with thinking. Sis Naajiní, Belted Mountain, is the name of our sacred mountain to the east. Today most Navajos call it Blanca Peak. This name is meaningless and has no connection to the true meaning of *Sis Naajiní*. Mountain tobacco is sacred food for our minds, for clear and strong thinking. In the past, people used to wear tobacco belts all the time, containing their mountain tobaccos, their pipes, and lighter. So, they placed *Sis Naajiní* to the east, wearing the mountain tobacco belt. So, the name of our eastern mountain holds all the stories, songs, prayers, and rituals that make our minds healthy and strong. We need to start reclaiming all our place names in Navajo. Our land and our people must become one again by uttering the names of the place where we live in our Navajo language, provoking intimate songs and prayers.

> I am my home. . . .
> songs of dawn arise in me
> blue birds singing among the
> ponderosa trees
> the sun rising, rising
> lights rushing among rustling leaves
> the songs of the wind waving
> through tips of pines
> whining in sunlight
> shining upon my face
> warming my cheeks
> warmth soaking me in warmth
> feeling all warm inside
> my home is in me. . . .
> breathing, breathing, breathing, breathing
> I am in my home. . . .
> as the sun moves across the southern
> sphere sunflowers rise, stand, and then bow
> hódzą'—stepping in day carrier's
> footprints

At dawn when the Blessing Way ends, the last song sends a young person on the footprint trail—akék'eh hashchíín bikáá'góó be'elnih—the way to a healthy, productive life. There are several, different last songs for this core ceremony. The first blessing way ceremony done for an individual, especially a young person normally has the footprint song—*keeyeé'éyóo kéeyah hózhǫ́*—as a last song in the early morning, leading to self-determination, independence, interdependence, and thus eventually to a holistic way of living. The song speaks of *kéyah*, meaning land, but what is meant in the song is the space beneath your feet—*bikee' bi-yaagi*. So, this is anywhere where you take a step, where you leave your footprints. Thus the Navajo elders speak of songs, prayers, stories of footprints—*akék'eh haschíín*. In other words, your life path. The next last morning song for the second Blessing Way for the individual is when he realizes that true independence means interdependence, that you have relatives who can help you. The song goes—*k'eyeéyóo k'éeyah hózhǫ́*—speaking to *k'é*, establishing and practicing healthy, working relations. The third Blessing Way ceremony for the individual ends with the song for friendship or partnership—*Naghaiye shich'ooniye haiyigaałeye naghaiyee shich'oniye haiyigaałeye*—speaking of networking, partnership, and team-work to move forward in life with assurance. The last song is reserved for Old Age. *Bine' yisháął*—I am walking behind it. I do not tell it because it protects me. I will tell it when I get old or sing it when I do the Blessing Way ceremony for an elderly person.

Early Grounding in the Ground

When thinking becomes unclear or vague, hard or confusing, I always turn to Navajo stories for clarification. When I do this, I think, speak, and act out of strength and confidence. I learned this early on from herding sheep, donating my sheep for a ceremony to heal a relative, collecting herbs and plants I collected from the land for medicine and food, painting on bodies and sand, and ultimately using my voice for praying and singing, connect-ing people with their land with their inner spiritual landscape, thus restor-ing them to balance, harmony, and beauty—*hózhǫ́*. As a result of this early upbringing, I am hard pressed returning to the land for knowledge of and experiencing life, of viewing my life and its accompanying experiences as positive and productive growth. I, too, as have done the twin warriors in the introduction above, claim the land beneath me, the land between the four sacred mountains, as my sovereign land. I, too, breath in the sacred mountain bundles as my own on a daily basis. In so doing, I commit myself to help take care of the land.

The deep ecology and relationship of place have been important sources of knowledge and learning for me. In addition to my early childhood ed-ucation at home, I went to the Rock Point Community School for grade school, where I learned much about who I was. This school gave meaning to what "community" is all about. The Rock Point Community School was an internationally renowned bilingual, bicultural school when I attended it. Learning to read and write the Navajo language was part of the program. There were a lot of educational programs rooted in Navajo culture as well: we learned to cook all kinds of Navajo traditional food, both grown and collected from the land; to weave Navajo rugs, sash belts, and ceremonial baskets; to do silversmithing and leather works; to make moccasins and cradle boards; and to learn about livestock management and farming. To do these Navajo arts and crafts, we went out into the community and onto the land to learn and collect the needed materials. We also collected local stories by having collaborative conversations with parents and grandparents, and community elders, which for me resulted in several publications like *Between Sacred Mountains, Navajo Farming, Living from the Land* and *naakaiitahgóó tázhdííyá*. Introduction to these forms of interviews, transcriptions of the interviews in Navajo, translations of the interviews, follow-up interviews, and repeating the same process over and over for a period of several years was good training in learning the Navajo language, doing research work, exercising *k'é*, building lasting and valuable relationships, and always connecting and basing knowledge and experiences to the land. I gained the trust and good will of the communities I served. We presented gifts like coffee, flour, sugar, and potatoes. In high school, I was graduated to doing interviews on my own. The elders even teased me, stating, "So what did our in-law bring for us to eat this time around." Such teasing meant that they were open and honest with me. The interviews became more and more detailed. The elders learned to trust me with their stories. These community, collaborative-based projects were my first introduction to learn to work with others. The elders and community relatives connected me to the land where I grew up, at an early age.

One community member was my maternal grandfather, who used to tell others that he is a young fellow and was not around when the events they were asking him about happened. He used to tell us about the creation of the wide cornfield with songs and prayers. Then he would flap our ears and say, "This creation of the wide cornfield did not take place a long time ago, somewhere far away. It is taking place right now. The greatest and most powerful garden in the world is right here between these two ears—the human mind." Indigenous knowledges are not planting in sand because "things don't grow well in sand." Perhaps they do. Even Navajos know that although we live in and make a living from the desert, there are many other forms of gardening out there in the desert.

One such garden is the Navajo hogan sitting on top of a mesa in the high desert of northern Arizona. In the nineties I wrote a short essay on są'ah naagháí bik'eh hózhǫ́ǫ́n as a guiding principle to live by, sitting in that hogan, where all my thoughts are engendered. I looked at each syllable in the phrase and attempted to define each according to its place within the phrase in the following way: *są* as old age, *ah* as beyond, *naa* as environment, *ghái* as constant movement, *bi* as according to, *k'eh* as principle/core action, *hó* as holistic, and *zhóón* as balance/harmony/beauty. Są'ah naagháí bik'eh hózhǫ́ǫ́n nishłǫ́ǫ naashaa doo then would mean: Walking on, may I be balance/harmony/beauty according to the principle/core action that moves beyond old age. In Navajo, we pray to reach a ripe old age of 102 years. The question then becomes, "What moves beyond 102 years, beyond Old Age?" It certainly is not us. We die. Our bodies return to dust, the air we breathe returns to the air, the water evaporates and becomes part of the moisture, and our spirit and mind travel elsewhere, and we will not know what happens to them until we get there.

Navajo Philosophy and Land

According to Navajo epistemology based on experience and observation, what moves beyond old age are the teachings; we pass on the teachings that work because we are passing them on to our families. A teaching that works for me today in this environment and situation may not work for me tomorrow in a different environment and situation. The mood may change, the weather may change, or even the colors may be different. What works for me may not work for others. Thus teachings that work constantly change with each and every person. So, są'ah naagháí bik'eh hózhǫ́ǫ́n is constantly changing, ever moving. This is why Navajo elders say that one of our greatest gifts is our ability to change, to adopt, to adapt, to Navajo-ize. When we Navajo-ize, we simply integrate foreign concepts into our existing ways of doing things to improve and make things better for ourselves and others. Navajo epistemology and ontology remain the root of our gaining knowledge, learning, being, and doing, while we accommodate the changes promoted by outsiders. Underlying all this is our ability to choose, to make decisions. Because of this philosophy, my approach to life has been one of adventure, risk taking, and open to learning new things, and constantly changing to fit the situation as they arise, never diminishing, ever expanding—doo nídínééshgóó k'ee'ąą nídílzhish.

Many Navajos define and use sąʼah naagháí bik'eh hózhǫ́ǫn in many different ways, according to the ceremonies they know, the places they are from, and their lived experiences, and how they would like their children to live. Some people say sąʼah naagháí bik'eh hózhǫ́ǫn means Talking God and Home God. Others say that sąʼah naagháí bik'eh hózhǫ́ǫn means earth, water, air, and sunlight. Let me shed some light on these as examples of teachings that work. Talking God represents forward thinking, looking ahead, and planning for it. This outlook faces east and looks to the future, and actually doing the work to achieve what one is thinking about. Home God portrays a home for eating, resting, for reflective thinking, learning from the day, gleaning lessons learned from past "missing the marks," and shortcomings. Forward thinking and reflective thinking are teachings that work. This type of thinking therefore is sąʼah naagháí bik'eh hózhǫ́ǫn.

Here are other examples of teachings that work. Let us take a look at earth, water, air, and light. How do these teachings work? Earth provides a sacred place for all living things, and according to Navajo epistemology and ontology, all things are alive and walking. Water validates the form and usefulness of each container it goes into, whether it is a cup or tube, or a human being or a bird. It does not try to change the container, including human bodies. Air energizes and gives life to all that it enters. Sunlight brings out the best in things and makes them shine, even a muddy puddle. So, the earth accepts and provides, the water validates, the air energizes, and the sunlight brings out the best in things. These are teachings that work.

Bringing back the humbling utterance of a prayer, sąʼah naagháí hózhǫ́ǫn nishłǫ́ǫ naasháa doo then must mean: Walking about, may I think ahead for myself and work for it, and reflect on my highlights and shortcomings and find out what still needs to be done. It also means: Walking about, may I provide a sacred place for all living things in my life, validate and support who they are, give them energy and vitality, make them come alive, and in so doing, bring out the best in them and make

them shine. What a lofty ideal! Są'ah naagháí bik'eh hózhǫǫ́n nishłǫǫ naasháa doo! Here are teachings that work that could be applied anywhere,
with anyone.

Next, let us take a look at the first syllable only for są'ah naagháí bik'eh
hózhǫǫ́n for further understanding, and relate it to a daily Navajo experience and practice. When I was vice president of the Navajo Nation, the
president charged me with health and wellness on the Navajo Nation. We
eventually decided to have a run across the Navajo Nation every year. We
called our run *Running for a Healthier and Stronger Navajo Nation*. The
first year we went east to west, from Alamo, New Mexico, to Gap, Arizona.
We asked our medicine men to do a staff for us to carry along the way.
They made one out of greasewood—*díwózhiishzhiin* with a "life feather"
attached to the end of it. We call this staff *są́ gish*—old age cane. It took us
several days to do the run. We started early in the morning with songs and
prayers; stopped along the way in communities where elders and community members blessed us with prayers and songs, food and stories; and
we committed ourselves to healthier and stronger lifestyles. We ran and
walked with the children, the elders, people with disabilities, and people
from all walks of life. We ran for and with the people.

One evening we ran into a small community to rest for the night. While
the community was welcoming our runners and celebrating the occasion,
two young ladies needed to speak to us. We delightfully accepted the in-
vitation and went in with smiles. We ended up getting a lecture for almost
two hours before they stopped. Stunned, we politely agreed to hire a medicine man to do a protection prayer the next morning. The young ladies
told us that they came from a traditional background and that their grandfather and other relatives were medicine people. Their main criticism of
our run was that we were carrying a baton made out of greasewood. "You
are never, ever supposed to do that," they scolded us. "*Díwózhiishzhiin*
is used only to remake snakes," they hissed. "You don't know how much
danger you put so many people in, especially the young children. You have
done so much damage." They went on and on for about two hours. Afterward we went to see a medicine man and explained the situation to him
and asked if he could do a song or a prayer for the run the next morning to
"correct" the situation. The next morning, the medicine man showed up
and did his traditional "correcting" of the situation. The two young ladies
showed up as well. Afterward, they came back and complained that the

medicine man did not address the situation, that he sang the wrong songs, that it was only a protection song, not those for snakes. They complained that their grandfather did it differently, that the ritual did not even come close to what they had expected. It was a protection song, yes, to protect the young ladies from themselves. The medicine man knew what he was doing.

That evening I talked to my support staff because they were worried and becoming anxious about the run. "Są́, Old Age, is 102 years old and often older," I began.

> To reach 102 years, you must be strong, confident, and healthy. The staff we are carrying is Old Age Cane with a life feather attached to it. Yes, it is made of the stem of a greasewood. We offer hard jewels to Old Age. We offer it to a greasewood bush. We have prayer sticks we use in Blessing Way ceremonies, and yes, they are made of greasewood stems. The Blessing Way is the foundation of our core philosophy, our outlook on life, our mind-set. We build our fire with greasewood bushes to keep ourselves warm, and cook with it to feed ourselves. We use finely shaped greasewood sticks to stir our cornmeal mush and to make our corn cake for our kinaaldá ceremonies. We use bigger and thicker stems as *honeeshgish*, fire pokers, to pray with in order to remain strong and protect ourselves spiritually. We use greasewood for digging and planting sticks so we always have food. We use finely shaped greasewood stems to weave with and use it to make blood sausages. We use greasewood bushes to build sheep corrals and summer shade houses to keep us cool from the heat. And, yes, we even use it as toothpicks to clean our teeth.

I concluded by saying that we have many uses for the greasewood bushes and should not be limiting it to remaking snakes. Besides, snakes are sacred and have their own stories, songs, and prayers in Navajo culture. That is for another time.

This story portrays są'ah naagháí bik'eh hózhóǫ́n in action. It is grounded in Navajo epistemology and rooted in daily Navajo experiences. Rather than chaining the greasewood bush to an extremely limited and misunderstood use, it must be expanded to cover as much ground as possible, to allow it to do what it was supposed to do, to enhance and enable a healthier and more spiritual lifestyle unto Old Age. I believe that inherent in this story is also the approach we could all take to learning and living.

We have learned how to live from the likeliest of desert plants. We indeed are of the land where we live. We are the land.

Navajo Matriarchs and the Land

Our history tells us that the land beckons us to be here because we are created here between the four sacred mountains. Let me share quickly a story I have heard on many nights about a great-great-great-grandmother of mine named Asdzą́ą́ Woo'í. She knew the land intimately and used that relationship to her advantage during the time when Spanish invaders brought fear to Navajo Country. One day she was captured and brought to a great bonfire in the middle of a wide valley. The people knew she was captured because they heard her from a distance. She was chatting with her captors and laughing away. When she entered the camp, she turned to her gathered relatives.

"Cheer up! Isn't it wonderful that we are all here together on this fine night? Normally we don't visit one another, but we are all here now. Let's tell stories. Where and how were you captured?" She went on and on. The tired and hopeless people were irritated by her remarks. "Who will feed us this well at home? We have nothing to eat there. We should be thankful to these kind people."

She cooked breakfast, lunch, and supper for her Spanish Conquistadors. She showed the Spanish where to camp for the night, where enemies would not find them, near water and good grass. She ran to watering holes and brought back jars of water for the horses. Afterward she pulled up and brought back grass rolled up in a huge blanket for the horses. In the evenings she unsaddled the horses and brushed them. She even unrolled beddings for her captors and rolled them up again in the mornings. In the mornings she saddled the horses and warmed them up for the Spanish. Then she rode one of the horses out in front to "scout for enemies." She yelped and did tricks while riding. The Spanish were entertained by her horsing around and let her try out different horses. She cared for her captors with great delight. She even teased them, "Come now, eat some more. If you get too skinny, your wife may not recognize you when you get home. Oh, you don't want me! I'm sure you've got a better-looking wife back home!" Other Navajo captives thought she was crazy. Perhaps she was.

Now all the Spanish began to argue among themselves as to who should take her when they returned home. Many argued that they would like to take her as their wife, and others wanted her for their sons or bosses. And I can only imagine how she flirted with them. What a lady!

This went on for several days. Finally, they came to a place near where the Chinle Valley Store used to be. To the west of this place is a red bluff that stretches for miles in either direction. And straight west of where they camped is a place called Bąąh Nijighas, the Place Where You Slip. There is no way up the bluff except for that slippery place of giant steps of sandstone. Even humans have a hard time going up, almost having to crawl!

My great-great-great-grandmother did her routine that morning. They were ready to move on when she got on this one horse and started out west, away from the direction in which she normally scouted. As she galloped to the west, she let out a scream that clearly challenged her Spanish captors, "Come catch me if you can!" Her captors immediately knew that she was escaping. They accepted the challenge and took off after her. Of course, they did not have a chance because each morning, when she warmed the horses, she had been testing them. And that morning she was on the fastest, the toughest, and the most surefooted horse that would easily dance up that intimidating bluff.

I do not know who was listening, but it is told that she said to the horse as they began up the Place Where You Slip, "Miss a step and be killed!" She made it to the top and escaped to Black Mesa, where she killed the horse on which she escaped for the people who were in hiding there and suffering from starvation.

You cannot love thy enemy unless you love thy self and thy country. I would love to dance with my enemies like my great-great-great-grandmother did. What confidence! What competence! What a woman! Of course, my greatest enemy is myself. Yes, we are taught to ask when faced with a challenge, "What would Asdzą́ą́ Woo'í do?"

There is another story that my grandmother and then later my mother used to tell us about my great-great-grandmother who was captured by the Mexicans and her eventual escape from their imprisonment. She could have easily escaped while en route to Mexico, but she stayed with her captors because they also took her ten-year-old son. Her captors never left her son with her overnight, afraid that if they did, she would escape with him. He was adopted by an ugly, stout Mexican when they got back to Mexico, and the boy started living well there. She also gave birth to a child who died there as well. She finally made a decision to return home after living there for almost two years. She escaped and returned to her land by following her memory of where the landmarks were along the route they brought her on. She crossed rivers and mountains and traveled with "wild" animals. One night she heard twigs and branches breaking under something heavy. "'Not the Mexicans!' she prayed. Then whatever it was cried out. 'Shoo, that's the voice of The One Who Walks the Mountains,' she thought. 'The Bear!' She prayed to that bear the way she had prayed to the river earlier: 'Grandchild, I pray that no enemy sees me as I go to my land. Though I have no relatives, though they all be captured, even so I go home because I long for my land.' Thus, talking and praying, woman and bear walked together through the night. And always the bear's voice answered her."

These two stories of my ancestors depict the taking of Navajo matriarchs from the land they love, but portrays their unwavering commitment to returning to the land that loved them. When the Navajos negotiated the treaty of 1868, Barboncito lead the negotiation.

> This ground we were brought on, it is not productive. We plant but it does not yield. All the stock we brought here has died . . . we have done all we could possibly do, but found it to be labor in vain. . . . For that reason, we have not planted or tried to do anything this year. It is true we put seed in the ground but it would not grow two feet high. The reason I cannot tell, only I think this ground was never intended for us. We know how to irrigate and farm. Still, we cannot raise a crop here. I hope to God, you will not ask me to go to any other country except my own. (Navajo Treaty, 1868)

Barboncito simply stated what *Diné Bikéyah* meant to Navajo people since that proclamation by the Twin Warriors from the zenith of the sky. *Diné Bikéyah* beckons all *diné* back to the homeland.

Fortunately, we still have strong mothers and grandmothers who continue to press on exercising what they know from their lived experience of their cultural heritage, who respond from a source of strength, confidence, knowledge, and faith. They speak their languages, practice their culture, and function as mothers, grandmothers, and medicine women.

My mother was a Navajo woman who functions out of her own heritage, her Navajo epistemology and ontology. She spoke only Navajo and survived and thrived by practicing her traditional economic sovereignty. In her younger days, she herded sheep, sheared, and made her own yarn. She wove rugs, traded them for her needs, and sold them for money. Exercising her epistemological sovereignty, rooted in *nihimá nahaszáán, nihimá nihikéyah*, allowed her to feed her children and provide for them. In fact, one time we were talking about one of my sisters having to go after the father of her kids for child support, my mother overheard the intense discussion and she said, "Leave the man alone. He belongs to a different clan. We don't need his money. The children are of the *Kin Łichíí'nii* People. There are many of us *Kin Łichíínii* here. *Kǫǫ́ nihikéyah, kǫǫ́ kééhwiit'į́.* Here is our land. Here we live. We can raise healthy children on our own." That put a stop to all discussion on going after child support. This is a Navajo matriarch in action, applying Navajo epistemology and ontology to a specific situation. We cannot claim individual freedom with a Western framework, but always act out of a duty to the community, from within a collective framework of "sacrifice" for the survivance of who we are as a people and a nation. Relationship is important in other ways as well in Navajo country.

K'é—building and exercising lasting and valuable relationships—is important in any society, especially in Navajo society. We create trust by hanging out with the people in their own environment. We become more humane and treat people with trust, respect, and dignity. Many ceremonies are sacred and serious. However, a great part of that seriousness is humor and play. Many grandmothers and their families play games like tsidił, the stick game, at Enemy Way ceremonies. During these games, the elders would tell stories of what goes on in the communities and surrounding areas. People are relaxed, playing, and depending on the nature of the conversation, in deep thought.

At these ceremonies, people tease one another and joke around as well. These forms of relationship building could become serious, almost like a scolding, yet done with humor. At one such gathering, I brought food to help out with. As I entered the shade house with food, one grandmother came at me with a greasewood bush, swinging and scolding, "You only come when you are hungry. Where are your girlfriends who should be here to help with the cooking?" She was dressed in all her finery of velveteen dress and turquoise jewelry. I ran out; she finally stopped chasing me and went back into the cook house. People outside in their trucks were honking their horns and others were whooping, clapping, and dancing, taking in the moment. I followed her back in. She came over and gave me a hug, "My grandson, how are you. Thank you for coming and helping out." She was all smiles. In Navajo, grandmothers treat their grandsons as if they were jealous girlfriends. That morning she enacted the jealous girlfriend relationship with a greasewood bush, involving everyone with laughter and delight. She reminded everyone that we need to stay faithful to our women, to make sure that they come to ceremonies to help in whatever way they could. These relationships between people become stronger and last longer through humor, and the teachings from the relationships cohere and stay with the person longer. Their forms of sharing are internal, become part of the ceremonial structures, and the information that is shared brings people together.

We all have a duty to one another demanded by *k'é*. We are responsible for how we interpret our interactions in ways that are respectful, reciprocal, and accountable. Fortunately, we do not have to stretch far in Navajo. We have the concept of k'é. It is important to know yourself as you move forward amongst your relatives. The Navajo "introduction" of clanship, the place you are from, your family members, and the ceremonial practices all speak to who you are as a person within a whole set of relations. This "introduction" allows you to learn about who you are as a person. You must be able to know yourself through this system, so you do not speak or write or act out of place. In a sense you represent all these forms of relationship when we speak; we are reminded of this relational accountability by this form of "introduction." First and foremost is accountability to self in relation to all involved. However, in order for us to succeed, we must also learn the concept of *ahił na'anish*. This teaching is about putting respect for one another in action. We all need to understand that if we are to succeed, we are to work together.

When asked if I am *Diné* or Navajo, I often respond that I am neither. I turn to the Navajo ways of self-identification and relationship building: the four clans, family, land, culture and language, ceremonies, and how we make a living. I am of the Red House People, born for the Red Streak Running into Water People. My maternal grandfather is of the Towering House People and my paternal grandfather is of the Spanish people. I come from a place called *Tsé Dildǫ́'ii*, Lime Stone Mesa or Exploding Rock when literally translated, southwest of Rock Point, Arizona. I am an educator and a business owner who is fluent and literate in the Navajo language. I also am an ordained medicine man who specializes in the Blessing Way, a ceremony that focuses on mental health and the restoration of the human mind to harmony and balance. I perform these ceremonies almost every weekend, and sometimes the smaller rituals every other night. I sing, pray, tell stories, counsel, and talk in Navajo on a daily basis, addressing the consequences of historical trauma and its continuing impact through the colonizing institutions that our people engage in. When people know these things about me, they can approach me in how to better serve them. We learn to help one another in meaningful ways, giving our due respect to such interactions. This way of knowing ourselves allows for a relationship bounded by family and the land in ways that demand exercising our collective duties to our fellow living beings. It is a reminder that we do not speak as an individual and cannot say anything we want for the sake of "freedom of speech." This is a collective duty and must be exercised with caution.

Healing Sustenance from Land

Personal anecdotes also are testimonies to the land healing an individual where faith and medical practices intersect. This give and take of energy life-forms is best learned when the plant people must die in order for me to live. When you know yourself through the land, you get to know yourself at a deeper level and become more human. The more and more human you become through your language, culture, songs, and prayers, the more you feel at home in "other places" and connect with those different from you. My younger brother was killed in a car crash involving alcohol. Although I knew alcohol caused the accident I turned to alcohol and drank away two jobs and a graduate program within three years, all because I missed my brother. Then one day I had a medicine man do a "cedar seeing" ceremony for me. These sources of diagnosis are hardly spoken of or discussed in finding the true causes of things: hand trembling, crystal gazing, dream interpretation, hot ember gazing, listening, star gazing, and singing and praying. Many Navajos know things through these activities and inform and help others become better. These "unusual ways of knowing" are often put aside as superstition, but they are related to ways of knowing beyond our normal sense of acquisition of knowledge and use of it.

The ceremony conducted for me demanded that I have certain ceremonies done for me, including which medicine man should conduct which version of the ceremony. All was done and I got well. One particular ceremony required eighteen different kinds of plants. Fortunately, I was literate in Navajo, having attended the local Rock Point Community School, so I was able to write down the names of all the plants. I became desperate because I only had two weeks before the ceremony and I had no idea where these plant people lived. The medicinal herbs were to be made fresh as well, not those that were preprepared. I went to my mother because I did not know the plants and I was frustrated. She simply continued weaving and said, "Go see your uncle." I did. He, too, simply smoked and continued playing solitaire. After sitting for what seemed like hours, he asked when the ceremony was and when the medicine man was coming. I told him. He continued playing, and finally said, "If he is coming in the late afternoon, we can collect the medicine in the morning of the day he is coming." I thought that the plants would be in different places with great distances between the mountains. For some strange reason, I thought all sacred and healing plants were in the mountains. He then said that we needed to go to the Lukachukai Mountains early in the morning to collect two plants; we needed the stems and the leaves. He drew a few more cards, grumbled about getting the wrong ones, and then said, "We will collect the rest on the way to your house. They are all along the side of the road that goes up by Smooth Rock, in the sand dunes and the small canyon." We did collect all the medicinal herbs the day the medicine man came, all within four hours. I learned the names, colors, stems, veins of plants, roots, even tiny berries, and later songs and prayers of these plants. He mixed some, kept others separated, and left some the way we found and collected them because preparing them was in the domain of the medicine man's responsibility. After that ceremony and having been healed by the plant people giving up their lives for me, my "sensing" the desolate desert turned the place into a lively and thriving environment, where I greeted the medicinal plant people daily with gratitude and prayers. Today I use those same plants, songs and prayers, stories, and rituals to help others heal. I have a healthy, working relationship with the "sensed place" where

I live. It is my home. Today, even when I travel, I long to be home. The land beckons me home.

> Escucho, y
> I try to hear,
> but shinitsíkees
> shił yanáaltał
> a multitude of voices afuera de casa
> de poesía takes me back
> to dogs barking in Navajo country
> reminding me
> aadą́ą́ʼ dibé náákah
> and my stomach growls
> dónde está carnitas con tortilla y roasted
> green chile
> escucho, y
> I try to hear,
> but the cicada like songs
> remind me of summer
> heat waves of northern Arizona
> y las sonas de lluvia
> me llevan a las nubes oscuras
> rising en la tierra Navajo
> mi voz rises, too

I love to travel, but wherever I travel, I always relate back to Navajo country just as the poem above shows. It was written in the jungles of Costa Rica, in Boruca territory. Yes, the land always beckons. The land is "the breath standing within" that moves us. I believe that we need to speak from who we are as a people, always connecting to place and origin, using our own languages. And to do so without being apologetic about it. Exercising our rhetorical sovereignty, our ability to express our own voices, to determine our own intellectual expressions, rooted in our Navajo-ness, is needed to affirm ourselves as a people becoming. Regardless of circumstances, change is constant, and we must learn to adjust to it. As such, I always believe that one of our greatest abilities as Navajo people is our ability to change, to adapt, to Navajo-ize, to improve on things we breathe in. It is this ability that sustained us so far. We need to continue to embrace change if we are to not only survive but thrive as well. Our clans, our stories of ceremonies and prayers, our dressing, our artistic expression, and our way of life demonstrate just as much.

Living from the Land

We tell our children and grandchildren stories not to necessarily remember, but to describe painful events as well in order to think about survivance, to learn from the past and move on. These collective memories tell of a cohesive and coherent evidence of a constructed and consistent application of specific U.S. laws. These colonial laws have failed Navajo country in ways that destroyed the relationships that the Navajo people had with their lands. These stories are lessons from the interactions of the land and humans. In the past, the United States has attempted to impose its many Land Management programs, which advanced disconnection from the land. For example, here in Navajo territory we have heard so many stories of the stock reduction of the 1930s that disconnected the people's economic activities, leaving them impoverished and dependent on the U.S. government. In the 1930s, while the U.S. economy was in a deep depression, the Navajos enjoyed "feasting" on mutton and selling wool and rugs here out in the desert. The U.S. government decided that the Navajos were overgrazing, supposedly based on scientific evidence, and imposed their stock reduction policy. According to the anecdotal testimonies, the Navajos had a special relationship with the land, and managed their stock according to the relationships between the land, the waters, and the animals themselves. When they had livestock, the grass was knee-high. The Navajo herders saw with their own eyes the healthy working relationship between the animals and the land. "The animals, the land, and the weather took care of one another," the elders told us. These testimonies of economic wealth and freedom from wage work were real, backed up by scientific evidence. These Navajos lived out in the land, lived from the land, and were well-fed and joyful.

When there were lots of animals, their hooves broke and softened the ground, and they shat and peed on the soil, thus fertilizing it. When it rained, the water soaked in and nourished the land. The elders actually herded the animals, constantly moving the animals to ensure that they did not gnaw the plants to the ground, causing erosion and runoff. They allowed the land to rest and the plants to regrow. Where there are plenty of plants, the moisture cools the air closer to the ground, and when clouds form, the moisture on the ground attracts the ones in the atmosphere, and so it rains. And the cycle goes on. Today the ground is hot due to a lack of plants, and so when clouds form, the heat from below and the cool air from above clash and create wind. Thus there is nothing but dust bowls. The stories told by the elders are true.

Today as I look west and see Black Mesa and clouds hovering above it, I see dust devils spinning out in the plains. Did we finally overgraze because we tried to practice what the federal government told us to do? I hardly see any animals out there, yet the land is suffering. I thought back to when my maternal grandfather used to walk the land. He would rise early, and walk or horseback ride the range land. He then would tell us where to take the sheep for the day, or chase the cattle to a certain area. Sometimes we separated the goats out and herded in different areas. We did not stay long in one place, maybe two or three days. At times he would instruct us to stay in one area among certain plants only for an hour or two. Whatever plants the animals were eating had to be limited, to ensure that they did not eat too much of it or eat it all. We learned that certain plants become poisonous if overeaten. Eating too much of the same plants could cause stomachaches for the animals. The plants also needed rest to regrow. If the animals ate the plants to the ground, it could cause erosion as well, especially if they started uprooting the roots—and the same with horses and cattle. They can eat certain plants when the plants are young or their flowers are at a certain age. We constantly moved the animals so they got the needed nutrition from the plants. And all of these changed with the seasons and the condition of the land. My grandfather knew the land intimately. He was part of the land. He was the land.

Land and Self-Knowledge

As I have stated before, I cannot emphasize enough that the Navajo introduction is a way of getting to know yourself. Once you get to know yourself, you can then get to know others. Self-knowledge is prerequisite to learning about and knowing others, including the land. For example, my maternal grandfather was a Blessing Way Singer, and most of his teachings were around the cornfield. He used to say that we are the products of our own teachings, that we are the product of what we think about most of the time and work on. He informed us that when we plant white corn, we get white corn; that when we put quality effort into what we plant, we get quality produce. If we plant and water squash, we get quality squash. From these basic and practical teachings, we gain wisdom when we intentionally decide on what we want to accomplish. The quality of time and effort we put into our projects determine the outcomes of our products. This means that we must determine what we need to focus on in terms of what we want and need to do.

Food is important to the Navajo people just like most people. Food is medicine. Food is becoming one with the land. We really enjoyed gathering plants for food. "These are medicine people, too. Treat them with respect," my mother would scold us when we broke out in laughter while gathering different plants for food. In the spring we would go for *aza'aleeh*, also known as *altsé hazlį́į'ii*, the first to come. We also collected *tł'ohchin*, wild onions.

> one spring
> i went walking
> holding
> hands
> with language
> she brought me to a bar
> of sand, dunes in all
> directions
> above
> an azure dome without
> a sign of dripping rain
> droplets
> she seduced me to my knees
> i caress green spiny leaves
> suggestions of purple buds
> want to burst
> dig them
> before they bloom
> sand dunes against sandstones against a
> blue arch

i kneel on both knees
dig deep with my mother's spoon
tł'ohchin, i dig out another
soon i fill a blue plastic bag from walmart
another bag and then another
the sun reaches its zenith,
sweats dampen the sand, from sand to dirt
mine
suddenly laughters of my mothers resound
in nearby smooth rock, echoing in window rock canyons
repeating themselves in the screeching of the eagle
spiraling into one dot, one black point
disappearing into blueness
language smiles tł'ohchin
tł'ohchin and she walks on
i wait with my family
silence
then a heart beats, my own
from the depth of silence
i look to the east and gaze upon a dreaming line
where earth and sky meet
birth of dawn
my child speaks

While attending the Rock Point Community School, we are taught many "traditional things" that we all need to take pride in. We learned about the Navajo Song and Dance that was held every year. This celebration was a competition between different schools where students were taught the various songs and dances of the Navajo ceremonial life ways. Earlier I wrote that the Rock Point Community Schools curriculum was all about local decision-making and empowerment, becoming agents of change. We were never told that the songs and dances we so proudly partook in were taken out of sacred ceremonial settings, which took place out in the communities, through the reenactment of a war ceremonial. The actual healing war ceremony starts at a grandmother's place and takes place over several days and across a vast landscape with singing, dancing, and healing going on all in between. These summer ritual dramatic gatherings were fun and exciting to be a part of. This was especially so when riding the horses from one place to the next.

Anyway, the school turned the songs and dances into school social settings and competitions all for the sake of learning our cultures and traditions. We did not know that these school learnings of traditional and sacred dances and songs were exploitations of our sacred lifestyles. They were exploitations of who we were as a people, extrapolating the sacred and what is for healing, for educational and language learning purposes in a different setting. Yet these activities allowed us to explore ourselves as a people and to engage in new ways to survive and thrive. After all, we are complex people, with multiple choices as a people who move on with options, hope, and resilience. Such measures may be necessary for survivance and posterity.

Other examples impressed on our young minds a sense of what was traditional. We had a duty to pass on; to wear calico and woven dresses, along with silver and turquoise jewelry. We were never told that these were Victorian-style dresses adapted from Bosque Redondo, and woven dresses from the Pueblos, and the silverwork was from the Spanish and Mexicans. These are some examples that we as Navajos need to know, understanding that we are constantly changing with the times. We simply need to ask ourselves when we are being colonized, being forced to adopt and adapt; or when we simply accept and change, accommodating the challenges of the day. As a people we need to acknowledge the past and move on to become a better people, with a desire to live on. Ultimately, my search is about finding movements between what does not work and what works as it relates to learning about who we are as a people as well as moving forward as a nation. It is about sustainability and continuity. Certainly, there is integrity in what we could pass on as tradition and what is not, or a combination thereof. We need to know ourselves through the bad, the good, and the ugly, so to speak.

The land is who we are. Even the land changes as we must also change. "*Ak'eego nahasdzáán bik'iní'diit'ood. Hanályį́įhgo yihah. Daango hanínáá-diit'įįh,*" one medicine man sitting in his wide cornfield explained, while harvesting the fruit of his labor. Whatever change we undertake, we must be able to sustain the integrity of who we are as a sovereign people and nation. *Sǫ'ah Naagháí Binehodzid* faces *Sá'ah Naagháí Bik'eh Hózhǫ́ǫn, ałch'į' silá* (they are complimentary and supplemental pairs), which speaks to this transformation of the earth, going from life to death and then back to life, that protects by instilling fear, awe, discipline, and respect (which will be covered in more detail later on in a different paper). As a people we have the ability to transform negative energy into positive energy, to honor the struggle, to learn lessons from hardship and move on, to exercise sovereignty with integrity and the necessary sacrifices. We need to move forward with a strong sense of urgency and our collective duties. We need to name, breathe in, and become one with the land just as the Twin Warriors did in the story at the beginning of this chapter, and claim stewardship over the stories we tell about ourselves. As the elders say, "They are all stories, simply stories. Walking."

In conclusion, Chief Barboncito stated that "black clouds shall rise and there shall be plenty of rain" when the Navajos return to the land. Now that we are back in Navajo country, we need to make sure that black clouds rise in the form of rhetorical, cultural, political, and spiritual sovereignties. We must create the "Indigenous critical consciousness" that Diné and Lakota Tiffany Lee writes about, learn from past experiences, and use lessons learned to improve the lives of Navajo people. We must allow the land to heal with us, so that we may once again enjoy economic sovereignty. We need to relearn how to take care of the land beneath our feet, every step of the journey, so we can all be healthy. Sometimes we may need to tread barefoot to make the connections to our land stronger and more intimate.

CHAPTER 8

On the Land That Holds My Birth Cord

JENNIFER JACKSON WHEELER

My mother's sunflowers swayed across the sunset over Blue Canyon. I was looking out from her bedroom window, noticing that the weeds in her garden needed to be pulled. She wasn't feeling well, but she was thankful. "Ahéhee', shiyázhí," she whispered, touching my arm. I took the warm tea from her hand and covered her.

"Íłhosh," I said.

Months earlier, I had just been accepted to attend the University of Arizona, so Rob and I moved to Tucson. We had a little one-bedroom apartment with stained carpet, dark brown kitchen appliances, and cabinets. "It'll just be till you graduate," Rob said. "You can do it." Mom was happy for me, too. Whatever my sisters and I wanted to pursue, she was always right there supporting us.

Katie and Lorraine, my sisters, were busy in the kitchen, their aprons smeared with tortilla dough and blue corn. Aunts and uncles were arriving, bringing in water and soda, bags of potatoes, pastries, and fabric. Cousins asked, "What can I do?" Katie assigned them throughout the dining room and outside. We had food baskets to be made, mutton to be grilled, and fruits to be cut. Everyone was helping and looking forward to tonight; all I was waiting for was Aunty because as soon as she arrived, Mom would be relieved.

"Cheii's back!" yelled Lorraine from the front door.

Cheii Thomas returned with his wife, Grandma Marie. He had sung beautiful songs earlier in the day before noon as Lorraine and I washed our mother's short hair with yucca root. Mom always reminded us that during a Blessing Way, we should feel comfort and love and k'é as we placed our feet, then our knees, then the palms of our hands on the soft sand collected from the cornfield. "You're reconnecting with our land Nihimá," she emphasized. "She knows it's you at that moment." She, like Grandma before her, liked to remind us that every natural element is a gift from Nihimá Nahasdzáán, our mother Changing Woman, such as sand gathered from the corner of a cornfield. At dawn this morning, Rob drove out to Crystal to dig up the yucca root. "Baa náá'jiiłnih," Mom told him, encouraging him to give an offering to Changing Woman before taking her root. The root was brought back, prepared, and placed with the fresh sifted sand. While Lorraine and I washed Mom's hair, I whispered in Navajo, "*Keep your hands there, Mom.*" Cheii continued his chant, and Mom, on her knees, leaning over the basket, kept her arms straightened and wept. That moment was hers. "Yee hwééhósin," my grandmother used to say. Nihimá Nahasdzáán recognized our mother, from the bottom of her feet, her legs, her hands, her heart, to the top of her head. When we were done, Rob gathered the drenched sand and placed the bucket near the door. The soft sun ray shone from the smoke hole above, onto our mother, her wet hair glistening, while Lorraine dried Mom with ground corn.

Afterward, Cheii had a bowl of hot blue mush and coffee. He had to leave. Grandma Marie had assisted some relatives with a Kinaaldá in Ganado, and she was probably ready to be picked up. "We'll be back this evening. *Have some mutton ribs ready,*" he had teased in Navajo.

Cheii and Grandma Marie were busy elders, helping many relatives and community members. Cheii was also Hashk'ąąn Hadzooí clan, from Sawmill area, but married to Grandma Marie, Kin Yaa'áanii, and lived near her Chiiłchin Bii' Tó community. Cheii knew our late grandmother very well. He apprenticed with Grandma's late brother, our old cheii, Hastiin Séí. Cheii Hastiin Séí taught many local men and women the old songs and ceremonies. He was well respected in our community and surrounding areas. Our grandmother used to call Cheii Thomas "shiyáázh."

Rob and I met Cheii Thomas and Grandma Marie at their truck and helped him unload some of their belongings.

"Straight into the hogan," Cheii said.

Rob led the way as we entered the cool breeze drifting through the hogan from the south window. We went around the stove and placed his belongings against the wall.

"Just put them there, shitsóoké," he said, "I'll fix them. Ahéhee'."

"Na', shich'é'é, here's some alkąąd." Grandma handed me a paper sack containing a large piece of Navajo cake she had received for helping at Ganado. I thanked her.

"Is there some coffee?" Cheii asked.

"Ao', Cheii," I answered.

"Hágoshį́į́."

"*Your grandpa didn't have time to eat,*" his wife said in Navajo. "*He picked me up this afternoon, then we went to Gallup. I wanted some Mexican food, but your grandpa just wanted to get his things at the hardware store. He said he was waiting for mutton here.*"

"Okay," I smiled. "The food's ready. We'll bring it over."

"I want to say hello to everyone, so we'll come over and eat at the house," Cheii said.

"Are you sure?"

"Ao', t'áá áko."

Rob placed some more oak in the wood stove. Mom's water bucket was within Cheii's reach. He was going to sing all night. In the bucket, the gourd floated.

———————

"Hey, babe, it's your mom," Rob said.

I had just walked back from class and was ready to make dinner. He handed me the phone, and I sat on the balcony of our apartment. Children were playing in the swimming pool and the adults watching them appeared to be their grandparents.

"Be careful, dear," the older woman said. The girl was covered in neon-colored floaties.

I couldn't wait to have a baby and have Mom watch her or him like that. The image of my mom holding our child was clear.

"Hi, Mom."

"Yá'át'ééh, shiyázhí," she said. "How are classes going?"

I wanted to tell her about how I was enjoying grad school very much. I wanted to explain to her how Beowulf is the longest poem ever written in English history. I wanted to let her know that I'm learning about the origin of bilagáana bizaad, the language that is unfortunately becoming our primary language as Native peoples. "Háádéé' shį́į́ yidiłgo," my grandmother used to say, referring to bilagáana bizaad, and I often think of her when I'm sitting in Introduction to Old English. Perhaps when Mom and I have more time, like the next time I went home to the rez to be with her, as we're sitting on the porch drinking coffee, or wrapping corn batter with fresh green husks. Perhaps then I can explain to her in Navajo how old Cheii Hastiin Séí appeared in my dream the other night. Cheii was riding his horse in the Blue Canyon mountain, and he came upon a bilagáana family at a wash. He noticed their wagon wheels were stuck in the mud, and the men were arguing about how to get the wagon out. When Cheii approached them, they were startled. They stopped and stared up at Cheii, and the folks turned out to be the Bundren family from *As I Lay Dying* by William Faulkner. Anse, the main character, was hauling his wife's dead body in an old coffin, with his children in tow. Cheii, in Navajo, asked Anse, *"Why are you hauling around your wife's body?"* Anse did not answer. *"Don't you know any better? Don't you know that you should return her body to Mother Earth within four days?"* I would share my crazy dream with Mom, and she'd laugh and tell me she has no clue what I'm talking about, that she's just glad I'm learning new things. "If that's what interests you, then good for you," she'd say.

Instead, I told her that everything was okay. "The walk to and from campus is short but agonizing with the heat. Other than that, I'm enjoying my classes," I said.

"Jó nizhóní," she replied.

"How about you, Mom? What's going on?"

She told me about her going to the laundromat and running into Mary Benally, who told her that her husband planned to host a five-night ceremony at the close of autumn.

"That's good," I responded.

"I know. She's been worried about her husband a lot the past few months. He's really going down physically, can't walk much with all the pain in his legs, keeps going to the hospital. They just tell him he might be getting bad arthritis and to take medication."

"Oh, that's too bad," I added.

She got silent.

"Is everything okay, Mom?"

"Yeah," she said.

"Mom . . ."

There was a long pause. I hoped she needed some money. I hoped she missed us already, so much that she wanted us home for the weekend, but Katie was home, and the grandkids.

The girl at the pool was standing near her grandmother. The grandmother was lathering her with more sunblock lotion. She was rubbing
some of it under the girl's arm, tickling her. The child giggled. Her grandmother kissed and hugged her, then she jumped back into the pool.

"Shiyázhí."

"Mom, just tell me."

"I don't want to, but I need to."

I closed my eyes.

She would say what I had been afraid to hear again for two years and
five months and a few days.

<hr>

When Cheii and Grandma followed us into the house, everyone was laughing. I knew it. Aunty was there. She was hugging everyone.

"Where is she?" she asked.

"Asleep," I said. I walked her into Mom's room. Aunty sat down beside
Mom and woke her.

"K'ad shíį hanééníyíį'," Aunty told her.

Mom smiled and hugged her. "Yes, I got plenty of rest. What time is it?"

"Nine-thirty," I said.

"I better get up before I get a headache."

"Well, I actually brought a skirt, just for you," Aunty told Mom.

"I'm already wearing a new skirt," Mom said.

Aunty laughed. "No, I mean for me!"

"Oh, wow, you're actually going to wear a skirt?" Mom replied.

"Exactly. I had promised I'll wear one just for you. The tight kind with
a long slit on the side, to show off my beautiful, hairy legs," she laughed.

"Doo ájíníí da. I hope you remembered to bring a slip too," Mom added.

"I brought a slip, and, of course, my long johns to go under the slip,"
Aunty teased.

"Daníchííl haniih." It was nice to see Mom smiling.

Aunty and I helped her up. When she went into the bathroom, Aunty
wheeled in her extra-large suitcase and threw it on the bed.

"Gee, Aunty, staying through winter?" I asked.

"You wish," she said. She unzipped her case, opened it, and exposed
two Pendleton boxes. "Shhhh," she whispered, and closed the case.

Mom came out of the bathroom, and Aunty told her to open the
suitcase.

"What is this?" She saw the boxes. "Did you rob the Tuba City trading post?"

Aunty laughed and pulled out the boxes and opened each one—a hot pink shawl and another one, beige.

"Wow," I said.

"So, which one do you like?" Aunty asked me.

"What? The pink one!" I teased.

"Okay. I knew you'd say that. It's yours. The other one's your mom's then."

"What? Aunty!"

"It's my I-am-super-proud-you-have-started-grad-school gift to you. Seriously. I know Mom's so proud of you, too. I can hear it in her voice when I talk to her on the phone. You'll do great. We'll all be at your graduation, front and center," she told me.

I hugged her and said nothing.

"You're welcome," she said.

Aunty placed the beige blanket around Mom's shoulders and told her, "It reminded me of the color of your ch'ízhii knees, so I had to get it for you."

I laughed.

Mom hugged her sister and told her, "*Your* ch'izhii knees."

The shawl matched Mom's outfit.

"Look in the mirror," I told her.

"I need to put my necklace back on," she said, glancing at herself in the full-length mirror. Her hair was starting to thin, again.

"Wait! Aunty, stand by Mom." I took their picture.

Lorraine and Katie came in. "Hey, what's going on in here? Party without us?"

"Oh, Mom. Wow." They admired her new shawl. I tried not to make a big deal about mine.

"So, guess who called?" Lorraine asked.

"My ex?" Aunty teased. "Which one?"

Lorraine laughed and said, "You wish. No. Mom's ex."

"Ha'íí?" Mom replied. "What did he say?"

"He's on his way."

"OMG," I said. "By himself, please."

"Nope." Katie shook her head. "Dad's bringing his sunshine."

Aunty is Mom's younger sister. When Mom and Dad divorced, Aunty helped Mom move on, reminding her of all the emotional pain he put her through for thirty years. During our parents' separation and divorce, we realized how much Mom really had been through. My sisters and I knew something was wrong often as we were growing up, but our parents hid it well. Mom did not keep secrets from Aunty, however. Aunty was across the reservation, but she was always a phone call away.

Despite the bitterness and emotional stress that Mom and Dad had to go through during the last court hearing, afterward our father still treated all of us, including Aunty, to mutton sandwiches at the flea market. Our parents agreed to keep cordial. These days, years later, our mother and father remain friends. Mom forgave our dad because she said he will always be part of our lives, that everyone makes mistakes, and that she ultimately has three daughters from her marriage to him. Dad, however, eventually regretted divorcing Mom. He told us that it's hard to find someone like Mom. His lady friends have been Navajo, Apache, and Hispanic. The most recent one is a woman two years younger than me, from the Sanders area, Sunshine Tsosie. Katie and I were in Gallup one weekend, and we ran into Dad and Sunshine at the flea market. Our father was talking to a clan uncle of ours, and she was standing across at a booth of Pueblo jewelry, holding a necklace of heavy turquoise beads. She was trying to get our father's attention, but he was talking with his brother. Katie and I went over to say hello to Dad and our uncle.

We didn't chat long when Sunshine joined us and said, "Hi, girls."

"Yá'át'ééh," I replied. I didn't know whether to address her as Sunshine or shideezhí or shimá.

"'Hi, girls,' iss! What's with the feathered hair and red Madonna lips?" Katie exclaimed as we drove away. "Someone needs to tell her the eighties are long gone."

"Calm down," I replied. "Never mind Madonna. What's up with the eyelashes?"

Cheii and his wife had steam corn stew and grilled mutton ribs. Satisfied, they told us to get ready, then returned to the hogan. Other family had arrived and claimed their seats on the earth floor. The last part of the ceremony for Mom was ready to begin. My late grandmother always encouraged us to support one another, to come together as Hashk'ą̄ąn Hadzooí family. Blessing Way is what our mother requested at her home. It always comforted her. It gave her strength. "Time to do this again," I had told my sisters.

Aunty was the biggest support. She was the first to donate. A nurse at Tuba City hospital, still single, except for the occasional Hopi boyfriend, Aunty was always willing to drive across the rez, through Kykotsmovi and Keams Canyon, to Fort Defiance and Blue Canyon, and finally to Mom's home. Aunty and Mom had only each other now. Their only brother, my late Uncle Jim, who was the oldest sibling, passed away when I was still in high school. Mom took it very hard when he passed; the three of them were very close. Before Aunty was born, Uncle taught Mom how to hunt for rabbits and wild turkey in the mountains near Sawmill. He showed her how to make her own slingshot and how to aim it. His cancer was sudden. It came and went like a fierce summer twister, taking him with it. Lorraine, Katie, and I enjoyed listening to Mom and Aunty reminiscing about him. At this time, however, no one spoke of Uncle Jim because of Mom's recent diagnosis. Her cancer had returned. She said all she had now was prayer.

Katie is the oldest. An elementary teacher at the local school, she is patient, kind, creative, and loves her job. Her four children keep Mom company all the time. When they are not at the corral with their father, Frank, they help Mom in her garden. Mom tells them stories about how she was raised on a large farm near Sawmill. Her father raised many animals, including large pigs, and he butchered one for the family every winter. She remembers the water boiling over the open fire and her father scooping out the scalding water, pouring it on the pig's skin, and scraping its fur. "The steam from the scorching water disappeared into the pines behind us," she would say. "Although it was freezing cold outside, everyone helped."

I could not wait to have a child of my own who would listen to Mom's stories.

Lorraine, the youngest, drove back from Albuquerque to help. "Oh gee, I'm getting rusty!" she yelled when she was cutting out the internal organs of the sheep the day before. Katie and I held the large bowl under the carcass, and it was getting heavier. "Yáa, hurry up!" I told her. My legs were getting weak. Mom was asleep inside as we finished butchering. "That's why you need to bring Clinton back," Katie teased her. Clinton, Lorraine's long-time boyfriend, from Isleta pueblo, had National Guard this weekend. They lived in Clinton's late grandmother's house outside of Albuquerque. Clinton's family liked our sister. She was comfortable there.

It was dark, close to eleven o'clock, and the stars were bright. Aunty was going to sit by Mom, then me, Lorraine, and Katie. I took my new shawl into the hogan, and Cheii said to let everyone know that he was ready. I told him I'll let Mom know, and as I opened the blanket hanging in the doorway, Dad's truck pulled up. I walked over to greet them. He got out and hugged me.

"Hi, Dad."

"Yá'át'ééh, shiyázhí."

I heard the passenger door close, and Sunshine came around. "Hello," she said. "I'm sorry to hear about your mom."

She, blinking with those ridiculous eyelashes, hugged me lightly, and I returned the greeting. I had never met a Navajo woman who wore strong perfume to a ceremony. I helped them take some groceries into the house. Lorraine rolled her eyes from the kitchen. Katie had no choice but to greet them first as she prepared gift baskets on the living room floor. She was going to shake Sunshine's hand, but Sunshine put her arms around Katie. Katie, noticing the perfume, glanced at me with slight disgust over Sunshine's shoulder.

We assembled the blankets and fabrics that family donated, creating a rectangular, layered pile. Dad folded the thick pile in half and then tied it into one large roll. He was being cordial and respectful. Aunty walked into the living room with Mom and said, "Okay, we're ready." Dad hugged Mom quietly, and we followed each other to the hogan. Rob and Dad carried the heavy roll, Katie the coffee pot, Lorraine the pastries, and I the paperware. Sunshine followed.

Aunty thanked Cheii and Grandma Marie and all of our family members who were sitting with us. She explained that we did the same ceremony for Mom over two years ago, that it had been a difficult time for Mom, but through prayer and family support she was able to beat colon cancer. The cancer had, unfortunately, returned, and Mom started chemo again. Cheii acknowledged the introduction and update. He said normally this ceremony would be performed at the end of her chemo treatments, but Mom wanted to hear the songs of beauty and harmony and balance, from which she would keep strong and confident. He then asked Mom if she wanted to add anything.

As the fire gently burned in the center of the hogan, Mom cleared her throat, the fringes of her new shawl rolling between her fingers. She introduced herself, clans first, then explained in Navajo, *"Thank you all for joining me and the girls here today and this evening. I'm grateful for all the love and support. Thank you, my uncle, and my aunt, for helping me. From the doorway, to the south, to the west, to the north, and back to the doorway, each and every one of you, thank you. My late mother used to say that we are children of the Holy People. They give us life. Changing Woman in particular gives us our identity. She is not just the land we breathe on, the land we live on; she is our mother. When we have Kinaaldá, for example, Changing Woman gives us corn from her belly, and we use that corn to feed people, to bless the Kinaaldá and everyone in attendance. On the final morning, we feed Changing Woman the corn cake by placing a small piece of it in the center of the earth pit, thanking her, acknowledging her. The Kinaaldá is dressed and molded as a symbol of her. The young woman places the soles of her feet, knees, and hands on the sand as her long hair is washed. She is at that moment Changing Woman. Changing Woman knows we are her children, her grandchildren. The last time I experienced this cancer, I prayed to her every day, every morning. I offered Changing Woman white corn each time. I said to her, 'It's me, your child. Whatever the plan is for me, I do not know, but I do know that I want to live. I want to be here longer for my daughters, my grandchildren, my future grandchildren. All I can offer you is this corn.' I prayed this way when the sun rose, before I left for chemo treatments. I prayed this way in front of my home, on the land that holds my birth cord. My mom used to say, 'Live your best life. Be a good person. Be respectful. Help others.' I do my best, and I pray. The Holy People cared for me the first time. I am confident that they will help me once more. Thank you."*

Cheii nodded in agreement and passed the pollen to his right. He cleared his voice and then started the first hogan song. The oil lantern's flames were bright and steady. Mom sat with her back straight, away from the wall. Aunts and uncles sang along while others hummed. Aunty and I followed along in unison, in prayer to the Holy People, in thoughts of good health and blessings, in hope of są́'ąh naagháii bik'eh hózhǫ́ for Mom. Our voices echoed Cheii's when he referenced the journey of long life in each beautiful hogan song.

Dad had always been knowledgeable about our Navajo songs. He, like Mom, sat straight and focused on the songs. His voice was loud and clear. I wondered what he was thinking as he was chanting along. Sunshine sat to his right, noticeably tired, leaning against the wall. She kept shifting and switching her legs underneath her. It's the thought that counts, my mother would say.

Halfway through the full moon night, Cheii ended the first set of songs. He instructed Mom to step outside and greet the stars and moon. When she returned, we took a break and brought in some snacks of fruits and pastries. Aunts and uncles took a break outside under the clear night. Dad also had gone out to get fresh air. Sunshine stayed, yawning. Katie and Lorraine handed out cups of fresh coffee and tea. I was helping Mom back to her seat when Aunty started giggling. I looked back, and across the room, Aunty was leaning over Sunshine. Sunshine was lying across the floor, legs stretched out, her upper body perched on her right elbow like a model ready for a photo shoot. Her legs had fallen asleep, and she was heading toward the door when she fell—in slow motion. Aunty said something to us, laughing uncontrollably.

"What?" I asked.

Then Aunty, trying to pull Sunshine up, continued, "I was going to say, 'Her legs are numb,' but it came out as, 'Her legs are dumb!' Can someone help us?"

"Okay, Aunty," Katie responded. "Quiet down."

Sunshine, hanging on to Aunty's arms, also couldn't stop laughing; she kept wiping her watery eyes, her arms weak and falling as Aunty was trying to lift her.

"Ge'," said Mom, embarrassed. Most of the family was still outside.

Lorraine put the coffee pot down and helped the ladies. They eventually managed to put Sunshine's arms around themselves and get her on her feet.

Lorraine tried not to laugh, telling Sunshine, "Um, your eyes. You should wipe your eyes."

"I'm trying to," replied Sunshine, fixing her face and hair.

"No. Your mascara," Lorraine said.

"Oh no. Is my mascara everywhere?"

Aunty, giggling, whispered, "Yeah, and your eyelashes . . . are missing on this side, and this side . . . looks like a comma, a hairy comma barely hanging on. . . ." Laughter continued.

Katie rolled her eyes, annoyed. "Where's Dad?" she asked, looking around.

Aunty and Lorraine managed to help Sunshine through the door. They gathered themselves outside, made sure Sunshine was not hurt, then returned to their seats. Sunshine cleaned herself up, wiping her face with a wet napkin, removing all her makeup. She fixed her seat before pouring herself a cup of hot tea. Dad came back in and sat beside her. He had no clue what just happened.

Rob kept the fire going, just enough to keep the grandmothers warm. Upon everyone's return, Cheii explained, "*Monster Slayers set out to destroy negative beings, beings that were killing the people. Monster Slayers were told, however, that certain beings needed to remain part of life. This included illness and disease. Imbalance was critical to the survival of the people. This illness that shimá yázhí has is an example. Hundreds of years ago, before the colonizers came, our people used certain herbs and traditional ceremonies to provide balance and wellness. Today, we are challenged with many things in this Western world. Many of our young people, our children, are losing the old ways. It's important that we all be accountable and value our cultural ways. Just because many of our children live in urban areas does not mean they cannot learn. They can learn our philosophies and songs and prayers. It doesn't matter where they are in this world, even across the big waters. Their feet are grounded on the earth, our mother. Changing Woman recognizes her children, her grandchildren, everywhere. We need to continue sharing these teachings and oral stories. So, shimá yázhí, you overcame this illness before. You can do it again. T'áá hwí ájít'éego t'éíyá. You know what that means. You will be well again so you can continue your journey of są́ʼąh naagháii bik'eh hózhǫ́ǫ oodááł.*"

Rob turned up the flames on the lantern. The next set of Journey songs began, and we followed. I wondered if Uncle Jim tried to hang on to his life like my mother was doing. I wondered if he simply surrendered to cancer and let the Holy People take him home. All I remember was giving his body back to our mother earth on a cold day, snowflakes slowly drifting over the greasewood around us.

Aunty checked on Mom now and then. "Are you okay?" she asked her. Mom nodded, her eyes closed. She held herself together very well. I was proud of her. I needed to remember to clean her garden before we head back to Tucson. I needed to remember her strength, her resilience.

Dogs barked in the distance. It was early morning, close to dawn. Katie and Lorraine kept falling asleep. They were exhausted. At the last break, they were excused. They wanted to start breakfast for everyone. "Keep it simple," Mom told them.

Cheii kept asking Rob to lift the blanket hanging in the doorway so he could see the early morning twilight. When it was time, Cheii asked Mom to exit the hogan and stand toward the east, embracing Diyin Dine'é and their presence. Aunty and I followed Mom and stood next to her, where she led us in prayer. We each joined her and asked Diyin Dine'é for good health, balance, love, safety, K'é, and happiness. We asked that Mom overcome cancer once more, for the last time, to give her guidance, comfort, and strength. Aunty and I finished our prayers, but Mom was still going. She was asking Asdzą́ą́ Nádleehé to keep Lorraine safe and happy with Clinton, south of Albuquerque. "You know where they are, where their feet touch you daily, along the river," she added. She moved on to Katie. "Let her and Frank continue to work hard and protect their family. Keep my grandchildren safe, let them continue to learn our language, and help them grow to be good people." Mom ended with me. "Give the same amount of love and support to my daughter and her husband Rob. Let her do well in school. I know that she and my son want to have a child more than anything. I ask that you provide them support and understanding, and that they will be blessed. I look forward to the day when we will welcome another little Hashk'ą́ą́n Hadzooí to our family." Aunty and I listened quietly as Mom renewed beauty all around us. Dawn Beings embraced us, and we returned to the hogan.

Lorraine and Katie did not keep breakfast simple as Mom requested. They brought in hot tortillas, scrambled eggs, hash browns, bacon, slices of leftover blood sausage, fruit, green chile, leftover steamed corn stew, orange juice, and coffee. Cheii and Grandma Marie were going home with full bellies. Everyone was served. Aunty and Sunshine brought in thank-you food baskets and handed them to Cheii, Grandma Marie, and our relatives who joined us and whose voices we heard all night through songs, stories, and prayers for our mother.

Everyone departed with gratitude and well wishes. Dad and Sunshine had to leave, too. This time, Sunshine, eyelash-less, was brave enough to hug Mom, who thanked them in return for coming.

Mom relaxed on her cushion while Lorraine and Katie took the dishes back to the house. Aunty and I started cleaning the hogan. I picked up trash, and Aunty swept. "Did I just drag your dad's new lady friend across the dirt floor last night, or was I dreaming?" she teased.

"I know, Aunty. What was that all about?"

"You better look out for her eyelashes on the dustpan over there," Mom added.

Rob was outside chopping wood. I finished folding some blankets and then sat by Mom. Aunty was doing one last sweep. I told Aunty that I was very thankful for her help and support, and I was certainly happy with my new shawl also, but I was most grateful for her always willing to be by Mom's side. "You probably even ditched your Hopi man this weekend to be here," I said. I explained to them that it's hard for me to be far away from home, in Tucson, far from Mom and everyone, especially now.

"Oh, don't be silly," replied Mom. "You need to do what *you* need to do."

"I know," I replied. "But sometimes it seems like I'm being selfish, like I don't care about you, that I should be here helping you instead." I held back tears.

"What have I been saying all along, all day yesterday and all night?" Mom asked. "What makes me most happy is to see all of you being happy. That means that you need to go out there and do what you want to do, shiyázhí. I am not the type of mother who expects her children to stay home forever. You all are grown women. You, too," she told Aunty. "Don't worry about me. Katie said she'll help me when I need help. Aunty said she can help when she can," she said to me. "So don't worry. Like Aunty said, we'll all be at your graduation. It's something I can look forward to again."

"Okay," I responded. "Ayóó'ániínísh'ní, Mom."

She hugged me and held me.

"I'll be okay," she said.

"I know."

Aunty, holding the broom, knelt by us and hugged us closely. "We will all be okay."

We held each other for a good minute.

"Why do Native women give the best warm hugs?" Aunty said, letting us go. "Love you both. I'm going to help the girls clean up."

"Hágoshį́į́," Mom replied. "Thank you, shideezhí."

"You're welcome."

"We'll be here. Leave the door open," Mom told her.

"Nice shawl," I told Mom. We leaned against the wall, her head on my shoulder, her arm in mine.

"Ni dó'," she replied, smoothing my blanket.

"Well, I think I'll go check on Rob outside. Do you want to go for a walk?" I asked her.

"No. Just sit here with me. Let's enjoy our coffee. You know I can't go to sleep until later, so tell me a story."

"Tell you a story?"

"Ao'."

"In Navajo or English?" I took a sip of my coffee.

"Nila."

"Alright." I put my coffee down. "Oh. I know which story to tell you," I said. *"Ałk'idą́ą́' jiní, old Cheii Hastiin Séí was riding his horse from Blue Canyon to Sawmill. He was on the old trail that goes behind the well. As he was riding along, he heard some people talking and yelling in the distance near the wash. Háísh da ádaat'į? he thought. His horse led him to the commotion between the pine trees, and it was a family, a bilagáana family. Cheii observed them for a while. Ha'át'íí, he thought. Their wagon was stuck in the mud, and they were yelling at each other."*

In our language, I continued the story for Mom. In our language, stories are powerful. From the doorway, the sun greeted us—its long, soft beam reaching across the earth floor, gently touching the soles of our moccasins.

Conclusion

Nihikéyah remains strong among the Diné people, with all its histories and challenges, and it will continue to do so for many generations to come. The Navajo Nation has more than 400,000 citizens, and Nihikéyah is home to all of them. Each contributor to this anthology and their chapter represent a piece of the puzzle regarding Nihikéyah's connection to the Diné people. The book chapters show that the land is beautiful; it is facing numerous challenges; has significance to the people; and will always be home to each person, community, and the entire Navajo Nation.

The Diyin Diné'é created this homeland and instructed the people to live within its confines because it was specifically made to always protect the people. While not every single Diné person lives within the confines of the homeland, it is foundational to their identity. The land means the world, and history shows how hard the Diné people worked to return to the homeland, even though some of the original home is not recognized by the U.S. government as part of the current reservation.

The land is more than private property or a commodity. It is the existence of the people. The land is a physical, emotional, psychological, and spiritual family member of all Diné families and communities. It connects to the people's understanding of humanity and what it means to live on this earth and world. The land has energy, spirit, and provides the necessary elements to live in harmony and in relation with all living entities on earth and universe.

Navajo writers Luci Tapahonso and Laura Tohe offer similar perspectives as the chapters. For instance, Luci Tapahonso shares stories of Shiprock, the people there, and the strength of the place. In her piece titled "The Holy People Lived Here" in *A Radiant Curve*, she writes, "The Holy People lived here in the beginning. They built the first hooghan, made the first weapons, sang the first songs, and made the first prayers. Diné language, ceremonies, history, and beliefs began here. This is where we began."[1] Tapahonso shows the existential understanding the people have of the Shiprock community and Nihikéyah, and this cannot be severed or taken from them. The people are forever interwoven with the homeland.

Laura Tohe indicates how she views and connects to the earth. She writes in "Dinétah" in *Tséyi' / Deep in the Rock: Reflections on Canyon De Chelly*:

> I happily step over into existence, into our canyons, our rivers, our
> mountains,
> our valleys. Sky beauty above and earth beauty below. Oh, how
> I've missed
> you. To think I was away for so long, and you were always there,
> waiting on
> the red earth to hold yourself open and offer to carry my burden.[2]

Tohe's words present the importance of Canyon De Chelly and the earth. For each Diné person, the land is home and home is the land.

While this book is not an exhaustive analysis of Nihikéyah, it offers individual Diné views of the homeland and has several implications for the Navajo Nation overall. First, the land is the foundation for Navajo Nation building. The Navajo Nation is facing numerous challenges, from health to education to economic development to public safety to cultural maintenance and to so many other matters. What the people decide to do to confront and overcome their challenges will involve their families and communities. The land is family and therefore part of the thinking, planning, living, and reflecting process on all future legislation, laws, and agreements. As stated in the Diné Fundamental Law under Diné Natural Law, it reads, "The six sacred mountains, Sis Naajiní, Tsoodził, Dook'o'oosłííd, Dibé Nitsaa, Dził Ná'oodiłii, Dził Ch'óól'į'į, and all the attendant mountains must be respected, honored, and protected for they, as leaders, are the foundation of the Navajo Nation."[3] Nihikéyah is always at the discussion and decision-making table.

Second, the diversity of perspectives provides the Navajo Nation with ideas and plans to sustain and protect the land. With more than 400,000 Navajo Nation citizens, each person has a vital thought, idea, and plan to contribute to the homeland's sustainability. While the Navajo government is of, by, and for the people, the leadership including the executive, legislative, judicial, and security branch needs to include individual Diné knowledge and skills to help create plans to overcome the challenges the homeland is facing in the present and future. Since the 1990s, the number of Navajo children graduating from high school and attending college has increased. The number of Navajo students graduating from college and earning a bachelors, masters, juris doctorate, doctorate, and medical doctorate has been slowly increasing. The Navajo Nation is creating a critical mass of intelligent, skilled, and college-educated Diné persons. Many of these individuals want to return home and offer their knowledge and skills to help resolve, battle, and overcome the challenges families, communities, and the nation are facing in the twenty-first century and beyond.

Third, Diné family narratives need to be recorded and maintained for posterity. Many narratives are of the land, family experiences, and the community. These narratives should be documented and protected by the Navajo Nation. The Navajo Nation, in conjunction with its two higher education institutions, Diné College and Navajo Technical University, need to archive this knowledge for posterity. While Diné cultural knowledge has been told and learned through the oral tradition, recording of the knowledge through technology should be considered and implemented. A Navajo Nation oral history program funded by the Navajo government should be at both institutions. These programs' objective will be to interview and document cultural knowledge tied to families, lands, clans, and communities. These recordings will be the property of the Navajo Nation and can be utilized to teach children the history, language, and way of life. In the 1960s and 1970s, oral history recordings of Navajo individuals occurred and are kept at colleges and universities around the country, including Arizona State University, Northern Arizona University, Fort Lewis College, and the University of New Mexico. While regional higher education institutions are able to do this, the Navajo Nation government needs to make oral history programming at Diné College and

Navajo Technical University a priority, and returning college graduates and current college students will be more than willing to help achieve this objective. By recording, documenting, and maintaining this cultural knowledge, the Navajo Nation in partnership with the homeland will ensure its survival for many generations to come.

Fourth, the land is the foundation of a Diné way of life, and all decision-making has to reflect this understanding. As stated in the Diné Fundamental Laws, "It is the duty and responsibility of the Diné to protect and preserve the beauty of the natural world for future generations."[4] The chapters in the book show the love each contributor has for the homeland and the realization each can contribute to the sustainability of a Diné way of life. While the Navajo Nation Council and president make decisions for the Navajo Nation overall, past decisions have not always followed the duty and responsibility of protecting the land for future generations. Going forward, decision-making, including those of the tribal government, communities, families, individuals, and businesses, should follow this accord of protecting and preserving the natural world including the homeland. If the government, communities, families, businesses, and individuals do not, the impact of environmental damage and cultural loss will be permanent and consequential. The Navajo Nation government has passed and implemented laws like the Fundamental Laws and a moratorium ban on uranium mining to acknowledge the importance of the land; however, more laws appreciating this understanding need to be created and implemented. Some examples of future laws include a grazing law respecting Navajo cultural knowledge and families; a less bureaucratic and more Diné-centric homesite leasing process; a sustainable economic development plan where natural law is the first priority; a public safety law ensuring the safety of the people and land; cultural continuation, including the learning of ceremonies, prayers, and creation narratives; language revitalization, where speaking the language is the number-one objective; education reform so students can receive a college and career-ready education; and health/well-being where many Diné individuals have access to healthy foods and wellness programs in their home communities.

The homeland and the people are interwoven, and this will never be untangled and cut. The chapters in this book express individual conceptualizations of Nihikéyah and the challenges the homeland is facing. Each contributor loves the land and being Diné. This love translates into the observations, thoughts, plans, and reflections about and on the land. More perspectives are warranted, and each one will display the strong link each Diné person has to the homeland and earth. Nihikéyah!

Notes

1.   Luci Tapahonso, *A Radiant Curve: Poems and Stories* (Tucson: University of Arizona Press, 2008), 5.
2.   Laura Tohe, *Tséyi Deep in the Rock: Reflections on Canyon De Chelly* (Tucson: University of Arizona Press, 2005), 35.
3.   Diné Bi Beenahaz'áanii (1 N.N.C. §§201–206). http://www.courts.navajo-nsn.gov /dine.htm.
4.   Diné Bi Beenahaz'áanii (1 N.N.C. §§201–206). http://www.courts.navajo-nsn.gov /dine.htm.

GLOSSARY

Ahéhee'   Thank you

Ahił na'anish   Working together

Akék'eh haschíín   Stories of footprints

Alką́ą́n   Navajo cake

Ałk'idą́ą́' jiní   Long time ago, they say

Ao'   Yes

Ásaa' Si'áan   Where the pot is sitting (area or place)

Asdzą́ą́ Nádleehé   Changing Woman

Asdzą́ą́ Woo'í   Woman with a limp

Ayóó 'áníínísh'ní   I love you

Bąąh Nijighas   Place where you slip

Baa náá'jiiłnih   Give a corn pollen offering before you take it

Barboncito   Navajo leader who spoke on behalf of other Navajo leaders during treaty negotiation in May 1868. He spoke Navajo and Spanish. The Mexican government identified him through this name. His Diné name was Hastiin Dághaa' (Man with a Beard).

Bá shíshchíín   Born for (father's clan)

Béésh Łigai Atsidii   Silversmith

Bike'ehgo   Is following

Bikee' Biyaagi—Akék'eh Hashchíín   Committing to care for all places we step

Bilagáanas   White people (Anglo-American)

Bilagáana bizaad   English language

Bine' yisháál   I am walking behind it

Cháálátsoh   Big Charley

Cheii   Grandfather (maternal side of the family)

Chiiłchin Bii' Tó   Chilchinbeto community

Ch'il Haajiní   Manuelito

Ch'ízhii   Rough

Dashicheii   He's my grandfather (maternal side)

Dashinálí   He's my grandfather (paternal side)

Dééh   Tea

Dibé Nitsáá   Mount Hesperus (Obsidian Mountain; north sacred mountain)

Díí Shikéyah   This is my land

Diné   The people

Diné bizaad   Our Navajo language

Dinétah   Place of the people

Diné Bibéé Ház'áanii   Diné Fundamental Law

Diné Bikéyah   Navajo lands

Diné Nabaahii   Navajo

Diyin Dine'é   Holy People

Díwózhii   Greasewood

Doo ájíníi da   You are not supposed to say it

Dook'o'oosłííd   San Francisco Peak (Abalone Shell Mountain; west sacred mountain)

Dził Ashdla'ii   La Sal Mountains

Dził Biyiin   Mountain song

Dził Ch'óól'į'į Gobernador Knob Mountain (Precious Stones; door-way sacred mountain)

Dził Łíjiin Black Mountain

Dził Nááyisii Sandia Mountains

Dził Ná'oodiłii Huerfano Mountain (Banded Rock Mountain; center sacred mountain)

Dziłk'ijí Bi'áádjí Female Mountaintop Ceremony

Dził Bízhi' Ádenii Mount Henry

Gáagii Bighan Crow's nest

Gad Cedar

Ha'a'aahdę́ę́' Eastern sunrise

Háádę́ę́' shį́į́ yidiłgo Wherever it comes from

Haajíínéi Baa hane' Emergence narratives

Ha'át'íí What?

Hágoshį́į́ Okay, alright

Ha'íí What?

Háísh da ádaat'į Who are they?

Hask'ąąn Hadzohí Yucca fruit-strung-out-in-a-line clan

Hashtł'ish Mud

Hashtł'íishnii Mud people (clan)

Hashkééjínaat'áá War Chief

Hastiin Adiits'a'ii Sání Chee Dodge

Hastiin Dághaa'í Barboncito

Hastiin Jaatł'óół Nineezii Sarcillos Largos

Hastiin Séí Man who lives in a sandy area or desert

Hayooł Wind inside a person's body

Honeeshgish Fire poker

Hooghan Home

Hózhǫ́ Beauty

Hózhóójí Nahat'á   Peace leader

Hwééldi   Fort Sumner (At the place of suffering)

Iiná   Living

Iłnáshjiin   Mountain Way ceremony

Íłhosh   Sleep

Jádi Háádi T'ííh   Antelope Lookout Point (Becenti community)

Jóhonaa'áí   Sun

Jó nizhóni   That's beautiful

K'ad shį́į́ hanéénílyį́į́'   You should be rested now.

K'é   Relations

K'é bee t'áálá'í dzizlį́į́'   We become one with all creation. We will care
   for the land for all living beings on it.

Keeyee'éyóo kéeyah hózhǫ́   Leading to self-determination, independence, interdependence, and thus eventually to a holistic way of
   living

K'ézh nidizin   Honoring kinship

Kinaaldá   Girl's puberty ceremony

Kin Łichíi'nii   The Red House people (clan)

Kin Yaa'áanii   The Towering House people (clan)

Łeezh   Dirt

Łį́į́'   Horse

Lukachukai   Patches of white reeds place

Másánís   Maternal grandmothers

Naaltsoos Sání   Old Paper (The Navajo Treaty of 1868)

Náat'áánii   Leader

Náayéé'Néízghání   Monster Slayer

Na'azísíto'   Cuba, New Mexico

Náhásdzáán   Earth woman

Nahat'á   Planning

Na'néelzhin   Torreon/Starlake community

Nanise'   Plants

Níchííl haniih   It's not snowing.

Nídíshchíí'   Pine tree

Nihałgái   Fourth World

Niháłtsoh   Third World

Nihikéyah   Our Navajo homeland

Nihimá   Our Mother

Nihimá Náhásdzáán   Our Mother Earth Woman

Nihodiłhił   First World

Nihodootł'izh   Second World

Nila   It's up to you

Nílsą Bi'ááд   Female rain

Nílsą Bikạ'   Male rain

Níłtsą   Rain

Nishłį   I am

Nitsáhákees   Thinking

Nihookáá' Diyin Dine'é   Earth Surface Holy People

Noodas'éí Dził   Mogollon Mountains

Saad   Language

Sạ'áh Naagháí Bik'eh Hózhǫǫn   Navajo matrix (various meanings related to living a healthy, beautiful pathway)

Sáanii   Matriarch women

Shábike'ehgo   According to the sun's travel (sunwise)

Shándíín   Sunlight

Shideezhí   My younger sister

Shikélátłááh dóó shitsiit'ááhji'   From the bottom of my feet to the top of my head (earth to sky movement)

Shimá   My mother

Shimá sání   My maternal grandmother

Shínaaí   My older brother

Shitsilí   My younger brother

Shitsóoké   My grandchildren

Shiyáázh   My son

Shiyázhí   My little boy

Shiye'   My son

Siihasin   Reflecting

Sis Naajinii   Sierra Blanca Peak (White Shell Mountain; east sacred
      mountain)

T'áá hwí ájít'éego t'éíyá   It is all up to your effort, hard work, and
      determination

Táchééh   Sweat house

Ta'neeszahnii   Tangle people (clan)

T'iis Sikaad   Cottonwood place

Tł'ááshchí'í   Red bottom (feet area) people (clan)

Tł'ish   Walking in the mud sound

Tł'óó'di Tsin   Remote Forest (Becenti community)

Tódíchíí'nii   Bitter Water people (clan)

Tó Bájíshchíín   Child Born of Water

Tó Dootł'izhí   Green River

'T'óó Bizábąąh T'éiyá Yee Yáłti'   They only spoke with their lips and
      not their hearts

Tooh   San Juan River

Tónits'ósíkooh   Grand Canyon

Tóta'   Farmington, New Mexico

Tówoł   Sangre de Cristo Mountain range

Tsá'ászi' ts'óóz   Yucca

Tsé Chį́į́h Łichíí' Da'azkáni   Red rocks

Tsédédééh   Medicine plant

Tsé Dildǫ'ii   Lime Stone Mesa place

Tséyi'   In between the rocks

Tsétah Tó Ak'ólí   Holes in rocks filled with water (community near Tsóodził)

Tsoodził   Mount Taylor (Turquoise Mountain; south sacred mountain)

Ts'oosí   Tsosie

Yádiłhił   Father Sky

Yá'át'ééh   Hello

Yee hwééhósin   She or he knows

Yilk'ol   Kinetic energy wave

CONTRIBUTORS

Mario Atencio éí Háshtł'íishnii nilį, Tódích'íí'nii yáshchíín; Ta'neeszahnii dabicheii; Tł'ááschí'í dabinálí. Na'neelzhiin hoolyéedi kééhat'į. Mr. Atencio is currently the Vice-President of the Torreon/Starlake Chapter of the Navajo Nation Government. His current research interests have foci around Torreon/Chaco Navajo history, climate change, Indigenous research methodologies, and Diné-focused transformative public policy. He is a member of the Greater Chaco Coalition. He is married to Kelly Francisco of the Kinłichíí'nii of St. Michaels, Arizona.

Shawn Attakai is Bit'ahnii and Tábaahá, married with children to Tó'Aheedlíinii. He graduated from Dartmouth College (B.A., 1995) and Arizona State University College of Law (J.D., 2000). Mr. Attakai holds Navajo and Arizona bar licenses, is a peacetime Marine veteran, a former Diné College instructor, and an attorney for twenty years in various capacities, including court attorney, associate, and criminal defense. Mr. Attakai is currently an attorney for the Navajo Nation Judicial Branch. Recently, he was a Yavapai-Apache Nation associate judge and Co-President for the Native American Alumni Association of Dartmouth. He also currently serves as the Vice-President of the Navajo Nation Bar Association and has developed the Four Directions approach, a methodology to conduct Navajo legal analysis using traditional Diné principles that set the Navajo Nation apart from other jurisdictions. Shawn believes in excelling at both worlds—thus he has studied Dine Bi Beehaz'áanii under several mentors over several decades and is a Diné traditional practitioner.

Wendy Shelly Greyeyes, Ph.D. (Diné), is Associate Professor of Native American Studies at the University of New Mexico and a former research consultant with the Department of Diné Education. Dr. Greyeyes formerly worked for the Arizona governor as a Tribal Liaison for the Arizona Teacher Excellence Program and Homeland Security, a Grassroots Manager for the Indian Self Reliance Initiative in Arizona, a Statistician/Demographer for the Department of Diné Education, and a Program Analyst/Chief Implementation Officer for the Bureau of Indian Education. She currently is the Navajo representative member for the New Mexico Indian Education Advisory Council (IEAC), President of Diné Studies Conference Inc., President of the American Indian Studies Association (AISA), and faculty advisor for the Kiva Club and the UNM Native American Alumni Chapter. Dr. Greyeyes received her M.A. and Ph.D. in sociology from the University of Chicago and B.A. in Native American Studies from Stanford University. Her research is focused on political sociology, organizational analysis, Indigenous education, tribal sovereignty, and Nation Building. Recent publications include an article for *Wicazo Sa Review*, titled "The Paradox of Tribal Community Building: The Roots of Local Resistance to Tribal State Craft" (2021) and a book titled *A History of Navajo Education: Disentangling our Sovereign Body* (2022).

Rex Lee Jim is of the Kin Lichíí'nii clan, born for the Táchii'nii clan. His maternal grandfather is the Kin Yaa'áanii clan, and his paternal grandfather is the Naakaii Dine'é clan. He loves to play with his grandkids. He works and plays hard for his vision to foster our language, traditional songs and prayers, and to ensure the prosperity of the Navajo Nation. Born and raised in Rock Point, a small farming and ranching community in northern Arizona, he attended the local school where he learned to read and write in Navajo. He attended the Newfound School in Asheville, North Carolina, and graduated from the Colorado Rocky Mountain School in Carbondale, Colorado.

He earned a B.A. in English from Princeton University, and an M.A. and M.Lit. in English from Middlebury College. After earning his degree, he worked with the Rock Point Community School teaching Navajo, English, and Spanish to K-12 students. He has published books and produced plays using the Navajo language. He is Executive Director of the Navajo Sovereignty Institute and Dean of the School of Diné Studies and Education at Diné College in Tsaile, Arizona. As an author, playwright, and medicine man, he continues to work on the issues of integrating traditional healing with Western health.

Manny Loley is ʼÁshįįhí born for Tó Baazhníʼázhí; his maternal grandparents are the Tódíchʼííʼnii and his paternal grandparents are the Kinyaaʼáanii. Loley is from Casamero Lake, New Mexico. He holds an M.F.A. in fiction from the Institute of American Indian Arts, and he is a current Ph.D. candidate in English and literary arts at the University of Denver. Loley is a member of Saad Bee Hózhǫ́: Diné Writers' Collective and director of the Emerging Diné Writers' Institute. He is also the program coordinator for Six Directions: Indigenous Creative Writing Program through Lighthouse Writers Workshop in Denver, Colorado. His work has found homes in *Pleiades Magazine*, the *Massachusetts Review*, the *Santa Fe Literary Review*, *Broadsided Press*, the *Yellow Medicine Review*, and the *Diné Reader: An Anthology of Navajo Literature*, among others. His writing has been thrice nominated for Pushcart Prizes. Loley is at work on a novel titled *They Collect Rain in Their Palms*.

Jonathan Perry is Diné, originally from Becenti, New Mexico, located within the Eastern Navajo Agency of the Navajo Nation. He has dedicated over a decade to serving the Navajo people. As a delegate on the Twenty-Third Navajo Nation Council, he represented eight communities; he also served on the Eastern Navajo Land Commission. He has also served as Becenti Chapter President and Vice-President. Aside from serving as an elected official, Mr. Perry has also been involved in environmental and social justice work within the American Southwest, specifically regarding Indigenous people. Mr. Perry is a leading figure in protecting water and other natural resources on the Navajo Nation and surrounding areas. Notably, he is most proactive in both preventing potential new uranium mining activities on Navajo lands, and addressing remediation initiatives for more than 523 radioactively contaminated areas from past uranium mining and milling. In addition, Mr. Perry is known for his knowledge of Diné Fundamental Law and emphasizes its incorporation into tribal government and policies to promote and strengthen tribal sovereignty. Through his experience in public service, Mr. Perry also works to address structural racism in the federal and state governments, and their programs that impact Native American communities.

Jake Skeets is the author of *Eyes Bottle Dark with a Mouthful of Flowers*, winner of the National Poetry Series, Kate Tufts Discovery Award, American Book Award, and Whiting Award. He is from the Navajo Nation and teaches at Diné College. He joined the University of Oklahoma as an assistant professor in the fall of 2022.

Jennifer Jackson Wheeler is Yoo'í Dine'é, born for Kin Yaa'áanii; her grandparents are Kin Yaa'áanii and Tó Dích'íí'nii. Originally from Many Farms, Arizona, she resides in Window Rock with her husband. They have two sons, a daughter-in-law, and two nálii. Wheeler's first language is Diné. She learned at an early age how to read and write Diné from her late grandmother. Being bilingual and literate influenced her interest in teaching Diné and Bilagáana languages. She received her undergraduate degree in English education with a minor in Diné Bizaad from Northern Arizona University, which provided her the opportunity to teach Diné culture and language and English on the Navajo Nation. After teaching for a few years, she continued her graduate education full-time at Arizona State University, where she received a master of arts degree and Ph.D. in English.

For the past twenty years, Jennifer has been teaching all levels of English, literature, humanities, and Navajo language courses at the postsecondary level while being instrumental in leading the development of educational programs and curricula for Diné language and culture in urban areas and on the reservation. She is a longtime educator and advocate of sustaining and revitalizing Diné language. In her spare time, Dr. Wheeler continues to write fiction and nonfiction about being Diné.

INDEX

Note: Page numbers in *italics* refer to illustrative matter.